Diesterwegs neusprachliche Arbeitsmittel
Aids to Modern English

Practise Avoiding Mistakes

A Practice Book for Advanced Learners

Part I: Pronunciation and Spelling

By
HANS BRINKMANN

VERLAG MORITZ DIESTERWEG
4121 Frankfurt am Main · Berlin · München

ISBN 3-425-04121-5

1. Auflage

Gesamtherstellung: Oscar Brandstetter Druckerei KG, Wiesbaden

VORWORT

PRACTISE AVOIDING MISTAKES ist ein Übungsbuch zu dem 1966 erschienenen, 1975 in 6. Auflage vorliegenden *Lernbuch* HOW TO AVOID MISTAKES. Der Wunsch nach einem entsprechenden *Übungsbuch* wurde schon in den ersten Besprechungen des Lernbuchs geäußert und in den folgenden Jahren von vielen Seiten immer nachdrücklicher vorgebracht in der Erkenntnis, daß sich reiner Lernstoff ohne die Möglichkeit der Einübung, Festigung und Überprüfung nur schwierig – und offenbar zunehmend schwieriger – vermitteln läßt. Der Verfasser war jedoch einige Zeit durch andere Arbeiten gebunden, so daß er sich erst in den letzten Jahren intensiver der Fertigstellung des Übungsbuches widmen konnte.
PRACTISE AVOIDING MISTAKES ist wie das dazugehörige Lernbuch in erster Linie für fortgeschrittene Lernende der Sekundarstufe II (Oberstufe) bestimmt. Es wird jedoch auch am Ende der Sekundarstufe I zur systematischen Erarbeitung und vor allem auf der Hochschule zur Festigung und Wiederholung ebenso nützlich sein wie das Lernbuch, das sich inzwischen fast ein Jahrzehnt bewährt hat.
PRACTISE AVOIDING MISTAKES bietet **Übungen zu allen Bereichen der englischen Sprache,** zu **Aussprache, Schreibung, Wortwahl** und **Grammatik.** Es erscheint in 3 Teilen

Part I: **Pronunciation and Spelling,** 57 Seiten
(zu HOW TO AVOID MISTAKES §§ 1–72)
Part II: **Choice of Words,** 68 Seiten
(zu HOW TO AVOID MISTAKES §§ 73–94)
Part III: **Forms and Structures,** 132 Seiten
(zu HOW TO AVOID MISTAKES §§ 95–120)

Part I dient im Abschnitt **Pronunciation** der Förderung der Sprechfertigkeit durch Hinführung zu einer richtigen Aussprache. Die im Lernbuch aufgeführten oft falsch ausgesprochenen Wörter werden im Kontext dargeboten, wobei die am Rand beigegebene phonetische Umschrift zusätzliche Hilfe leistet. Im Kapitel 'Word stress' werden Wörter gleicher Silbenzahl aber verschiedener Betonung sowie Schwierigkeiten in der Betonung ähnlicher Wörter behandelt. Im Kapitel 'Sounds and their spelling' werden die verschiedenen Aussprachemöglichkeiten von *a, e, i, o, u; g, ch, qu, s, th* sowie *silent consonants* und wegen ihrer Ähnlichkeit schwierige Wörter geübt. – Der Abschnitt **Spelling** ist unterteilt in 'Difficult words', 'Spelling of inflected and derived forms' (final silent -e, final -y, doubling of final consonants, etc.) und 'Special problems of orthography' (capital letters, hyphen, division of words, comma).

Part II soll helfen, Fehler in der Wortwahl zu vermeiden; auf einem Gebiet, das für die Kommunikationsfähigkeit von immenser Bedeutung ist und dem im modernen Englischunterricht zu Recht ein immer größerer Platz eingeräumt wird. Im Mittelpunkt steht ein reichliches Übungsangebot zu 'Synonyms' und 'Prepositions'; behandelt werden ferner 'Homophones, homonyms, homographs' und 'Cognate, frequently confused words' verschiedener Wortarten, ebenso wie die durch ihre scheinbare Kongruenz zwischen Mutter- und Zielsprache zu falschem Gebrauch verführenden 'Misleading words' *(false friends)*.

Part III bietet Übungen zu allen wesentlichen Abschnitten der Grammatik, insbesondere zu 'Auxiliary verbs', 'Tenses' (past and perfect tenses, simple or continuous; future; reported speech), 'Conditional clauses', 'Infinitive', '-ing Forms', 'Pronouns'; ferner auch zu 'Articles', 'Gender and number', 'Adjectives and adverbs', 'Verbs and their complements', 'Conjunctions' und 'Word order'. Jede Übung beginnt nicht wie sonst vielfach üblich lediglich

vorbereitung und -lenkung wird die Unterrichtsarbeit und auch die selbständige Arbeit des Lernenden wesentlich erleichtern und zu besseren Ergebnissen führen.
Die **Einteilung in §§** und die weitere Unterteilung durch Ziffern ist mit der im Lernbuch identisch, so daß entsprechende Abschnitte leicht aufzufinden sind. Hinsichtlich der Übungsinhalte besteht ebenfalls weitgehende Übereinstimmung, nur gelegentlich werden im Hinblick auf das gesprochene Englisch bestimmte Schwerpunkte gesetzt und weniger Wichtiges verkürzt. Phonetische Umschrift, Schreibung (Bindestrich), Regelformulierungen usw. schliessen sich an die 6. Auflage von HOW TO AVOID MISTAKES an; die Änderungen gegenüber früheren Auflagen sind jedoch geringfügig.
Alle zu übenden Wörter, Formen und Strukturen stehen grundsätzlich im **Kontext**, und zwar zunächst in kürzeren Einheiten, Sätzen bzw. Minisituationen, damit die ganze Breite einer sprachlichen Erscheinung in den wichtigsten Varianten ohne Beschränkung durch ein einheitliches Thema dargelegt werden kann. Anschließend werden sie in den größeren **situativen Zusammenhang** eines **Dialogs** oder eines **narrativen Textes** gestellt. Da die Texte jeweils mehrere sprachliche Erscheinungen erfassen, ergibt sich für den Lernenden über die bloße Wiederholung hinaus eine neue Aufgabenstellung.
Bei allen Texten kommt es nicht darauf an, Informationen anzubieten, sondern den Übungsstoff in angemessener Kürze in einen sinnvollen Zusammenhang zu bringen. Daß für einen bestimmten Übungszweck geeignete fremde Originaltexte kaum und unter dem Gesichtspunkt zielgerechter Konzentration fast gar nicht zu finden sind, braucht nicht besonders erwähnt zu werden; sie konnten nur gelegentlich als inhaltliche Basis dienen. Weil daher fast alle Texte neu zu gestalten waren, konnten auch unnötige lexikalische und andere **Schwierigkeiten vermieden** und versucht werden, eine gewisse **Motivation** durch humorvolle Situationen zu erreichen.
Da die Vermeidung von Fehlern oberstes Ziel ist, sind die Übungen ihrer Art nach vornehmlich lernsichere **Einsetz- und Umformungsübungen**. Auf Übersetzungen mit all ihren zusätzlichen Fehlerquellen wurde fast gänzlich verzichtet. Wo einzelne deutsche Wörter durch englische zu ersetzen sind, haben sie nur punktuellen Hinweischarakter. Trotzdem wird das **kontrastive Prinzip** in der Anlage der Übungen, Erläuterungen usw. immer im Auge behalten, um muttersprachlichen Interferenzen nach Möglichkeit vorzubeugen. Auch der intralingualen Interferenz wird durch Konfrontation in Minimalpaaren und weiteren Gegenüberstellungen bei bekannten Fehlerquellen weitgehend Rechnung getragen.
Das Übungsangebot sollte quantitativ sowohl für die **erste Einübung** als auch für eine **spätere Wiederholung** ausreichen. Eine **Differenzierung** der Übungen für mehr oder weniger Fortgeschrittene wird in Part II bei den Synonymen und den häufig verwechselten Wörtern, sowie in Part III hinsichtlich Schwierigkeit und Nützlichkeit durch entsprechende Kennzeichnung ermöglicht. Die **Reihenfolge** der Durchnahme der Abschnitte ist **beliebig**, in Part III besteht jedoch innerhalb der Abschnitte ein gewisser Aufbau, der die Behandlung der einleitenden Übungen bei den späteren voraussetzt.
Die Übungen sind sowohl für den **Unterricht** in der Schule als auch für die häusliche Tätigkeit geeignet. Für die Erleichterung der **selbständigen Arbeit** sind mehrere Hilfen vorhanden, vor allem die entsprechenden Abschnitte des Lernbuchs HOW TO AVOID MISTAKES zur Vorbereitung und zum Nachschlagen, ferner innerhalb des Übungsbuchs in Part I die beigegebene phonetische Umschrift, in Part II bei den Synonymen die Einteilung in *a* und *b sections,* in Part III die jede Übung einleitenden Beispiele und Erläuterungen, sowie ein Schlüssel für die ersten Sätze jeder Übung.
Für die sprachliche Überprüfung des Manuskripts und weitere wertvolle Hinweise ist der Verfasser seinen Kollegen Mr Bryan Garratt, Coventry, *(bei Teil I u. II),* und Mr Oliver Gray, Bristol, z.Zt. Bremen, (bei *Teil II u. III*), zu großem Dank verpflichtet. Für trotz aller Bemühungen auftretende Mängel ist der Verfasser allein verantwortlich.

Hinweise für die Arbeit mit Part I

I. Pronunciation

Bei einem Übungsbuch für fortgeschrittene Lerner kann davon ausgegangen werden, daß die zu übenden, nach Wertigkeitsstufen ausgewählten Wörter (s. Vorwort des Lernbuchs) größtenteils bekannt oder zumindest schon irgendwie vorgekommen sind. Es empfiehlt sich daher, die Bekanntschaft mit Hilfe der entsprechenden §§ im Lernbuch, wo Wörter gleicher Betonung oder Lautung zusammengeordnet sind, durch lautes Lesen wieder aufzufrischen, bevor man an die Übungen herangeht, die nach anderen Kriterien aufgebaut sind und die die Kenntnis der unterschiedlichen Betonung oder Lautung von Wörtern gleicher Silbenzahl bzw. gleicher oder ähnlicher Schreibung (hinsichtlich bestimmter Vokale, Diphthonge oder Konsonanten) vermitteln sollen.
Das Übungsbuch stellt die Unterscheidungen jeweils formelhaft an den Anfang, z.B. bei *Words of two syllables: ˊ– or –ˊ* oder bei der Schreibung *a* die verschiedenen Aussprachemöglichkeiten, wobei die §§ des Lernbuchs je nach Häufigkeit der jeweiligen Lautung in halbfetter oder normaler Schrift oder in Klammern hinzugefügt sind. Die Übungen beginnen dann im Kapitel 'Word stress' mit einer Zusammenstellung ähnlicher Wörter, im Kapitel 'Sounds and their spelling' mit *Find the 'odd man out'* als Vorübung, bei der die angegebenen §§ des Lernbuchs wieder zu Rate gezogen werden können. Die dann folgenden kleineren und größeren Einheiten unter b) *Situational Practice* dienen der Einprägung der richtigen Lautung der Wörter im Kontext. In der Erkenntnis, daß Fehlerprophylaxe jeder nachträglichen Therapie von Fehlern vorzuziehen ist, wird jedem zu übenden Wort (kursiv) und darüber hinaus weiteren fehlerträchtigen Wörtern die phonetische Umschrift beigegeben. Der Lernende sollte sich auf jeden Fall mit jedem Wort und seiner Umschrift ausreichend, gegebenenfalls in häuslicher Vorbereitung, befassen, bevor er die Texte laut liest. Wer schon an dieser Stelle Leistungsmessung vornehmen möchte, sollte die Randspalte abdecken.
Im Kapitel 'Sounds and their spelling' schließt sich jeweils noch unter c) eine Diskriminationsübung an, in der der Lernende nunmehr aus der Kenntnis der richtigen Lautung heraus in Form einer Leistungsmessung Wörter partiell gleicher Schreibung in Gruppen verschiedener Aussprache aufteilen soll. Es empfiehlt sich, die Wörter in Gruppen hinzuschreiben und anschließend wieder, wie immer, laut zu lesen.
Den a)- und c)-Übungen liegt dem Übungscharakter entsprechend immer nur eine Aussprache, nämlich die britische als die an deutschen Schulen häufiger gelehrte zugrunde, in den b)-Übungen wird auch die amerikanische angegeben. Beide Aussprachen sind an sich gleichwertig; gewarnt werden muß aber vor Normvermischung, d.h. vor der Übernahme von Varianten des einen 'national standard' in eine im übrigen ganz nach dem anderen 'standard' orientierte Sprache.

II. Spelling

Wie die Erfahrung gezeigt hat, lassen sich bei sorgfältiger Durchnahme dieses Abschnittes am leichtesten Fehler vermeiden. Die Gegenüberstellung von Paaren oder Gruppen im Lernbuch in Verbindung mit den dazugehörigen Übungen läßt die Unterschiede in der Schreibung deutlich werden und die Zahl dieser meist nicht schwerwiegenden, aber doch störenden Fehler zurücktreten. Wo es nur um die Schreibung von in ihrer Bedeutung nicht zweifelhaften Wörtern geht, konnte im Interesse der Kürze auf den Kontext verzichtet werden.
Was für alle Teile gilt, ist hier von besonderer Bedeutung: Der Lernende sollte die Lösungen nicht in die Lücken im Übungsbuch eintragen und es damit für sich oder für andere in Zukunft unbrauchbar machen, sondern die Wörter als ganze auf einen beliebigen Arbeitsbogen schreiben.

CONTENTS

I.

PRONUNCIATION

A. Word Stress

1. Words of Two Syllables: ´– or –´ ? 1,6

Read aloud (after you have read aloud the English words in §§ 1 and 6 of HOW TO AVOID MISTAKES).

a) Similar Words

1. accord – access – account
   aspect – assent
   collapse – colleague
   combat – comfort – commerce
   concert – concern – concept
   district – to dispute
   effort – effect – affair
   extreme – expert – exile
   mistake – mischief – to misprint
   product – profit – proverb – province
   purchase – purpose
   refuge – review
2. address – process – congress – princess – success
   advice – concise – precise
   patron – season – sermon – balloon
   critic – antique – technique
   aspect – effect – prospect – insect – direct
   fatigue – colleague
   agent – comment – content – patent – fragment
   distinct – instinct
   essence – immense – intense – licence – sentence
3. creature – mature – figure – future
   depot – despot
   palace – police – menace – preface – surface
   garage – image – prestige – refuge
   moustache – monarch
   to destine – doctrine – medicine – machine – famine
   crusade – decade – blockade – parade
   rival – legal – canal – petrol – hotel
   salad – solid – stupid
   April – July – August

b) Situational Practice

1. The pros and cons of Britain's membership in the Common Market, problems of *vital*[1] importance to British trade and *commerce*[2], were dealt with in *detail*[3] in a BBC *programme*[4] in *April*[5].
2. The celebration of the king's birthday began with a *parade*[6]

[1] ['vaitl] [2] ['kɔməːs]
[3] ['diːteil, *Am.* -´]
[4] ['prəugræm] [5] ['eiprl]
[6] [pə'reid]

of the guard, at the end of which thousands of colourful *balloons*[7] were sent up into the air. In the afternoon there was a *concert*[8] on the *terrace*[9] of the *palace*[10].

[7] [bə'lu:n(z)] [8] ['kɔnsət] [9] ['terəs] [10] ['pælis]

3. Followed by two policemen the *secret*[11] *agent*[12] ran across the street and into a garden without regarding the sign saying 'No *trespassing*'[13]. He knew that the only *access*[14] to the house was through the garden.

[11] ['si:krət] [12] ['eidʒnt] [13] ['trespəsiŋ] [14] ['ækses]

4. In *July*[15] and *August*[16] we travelled by *canoe*[17] along the rivers and *canals*[18] of East Anglia. One day, standing in the *canoe*[17], John lost his *balance*[19] and fell into the water. When he came up to the *surface*[20] again, he was covered with brown mud of a very unpleasant *odour*[21].

[15] [dʒu:'lai] [16] ['ɔ:gəst] [17] [kə'nu:] [18] [kə'næl(z)] [19] ['bæləns] [20] ['sə:fis] [21] ['əudə]

5. When a bill has passed the House of Commons and the House of Lords, it is sent to the *sovereign*[22] for the Royal *Assent*[23]. The last *monarch*[24] who refused *assent*[23] to a parliamentary[25] bill was Queen Anne in 1707.

[22] ['sɔvrin] [23] [ə'sent] [24] ['mɔnək] [25] [ˌpɑ:lə'mentri]

6. At the *banquet*[26] the president *addressed*[27] the ambassadors[28] and made some *concise*[29] *comments*[30] upon the *prospect*[31] of abolishing[32] nuclear[33] weapons[34].

[26] ['bæŋkwit] [27] [ə'dres(t)] [28] [æm'bæsədə(z)] [29] [kən'sais] [30] ['kɔment(s)] [31] ['prɔspekt] [32] [ə'bɔliʃiŋ] [33] ['nju:kliə] [34] ['wepən(z)]

7. After England had declared a *blockade*[35] of the German coast in 1914, Germany declared a similar *blockade*[35] of England and began the submarine warfare[36] by which she lost a lot of her national *prestige*[37].

[35] [blɔ'keid] [36] ['wɔ:fɛə] [37] [pre'sti:ʒ]

8. The *critics*[38] were of the opinion that the young *artist's*[39] *talent*[40] for *sculpture*[41] did not *accord*[42] with his *mature*[43] mastery of *portrait*[44] painting.

[38] ['kritik(s)] [39] ['ɑ:tist(s)] [40] ['tælənt] [41] ['skʌlptʃə] [42] [ə'kɔ:d] [43] [mə'tjuə, mə'tʃuə] [44] ['pɔ:trit]

9. Some *proverbs*[45]: *Constant*[46] dripping wears away the stone. – *Content*[47] is oftener found in the cottage than in the *palace*[48]. – Wise men learn by other men's *mistakes*[49]; fools, by their own.

[45] ['prɔvə:b(z)] [46] ['kɔnstənt] [47] [kən'tənt] [48] ['pælis] [49] [mis'teik(s)]

Cybernetics[1] and the Use of Computers[2]

In an article in the 'New Statesman' (Dec. 1968) Mr Anthony Wedgewood Benn, then Minister of Technology[3], said about cybernetics and the use of computers: "There is not a single *aspect*[4] of life that will not be deeply touched by it. The *effect*[5] of this will be far-reaching on both government and society over the next *decade*[6]."

[1] [ˌsaibə:'netiks] [2] [kəm'pju:tə(z)] [3] [tek'nɔlədʒi] [4] ['æspekt] [5] [i'fekt] [6] ['dekeid]

A computer can only be used when it has been programmed with the information it needs to perform its job; so computer people will have to ask questions about everything. This *process*[7] of interrogation, however, is both valuable and *extremely*[8] troubling, for "the acquisition of more information and its storage in centralised form, with unlimited *access*[9] by government departments or *private*[10] firms, would, without safeguards[11], pose a *direct*[12] threat[13] to individual liberty. This has been the subject of serious *concern*[14] for some time and there is little doubt that new constitutional safeguards will be required sooner or later to protect the individual as these systems develop".

[7] ['prəusəs, *Am.* 'prɔ~] [8] [iks'tri:mli] [9] ['ækses] [10] ['praivit] [11] ['seifgɑ:d(z)] [12] [di'rekt, dai~] [13] [θret] [14] [kən'sə:n]

Richard the Lionheart

During the Third *Crusade*[1], before the end of the *campaign*[2], Richard the Lionheart set sail for England. A storm, however, did a lot of *mischief*[3] to his small fleet, and he was shipwrecked in the Adriatic[4]. On his way across the Continent he was captured by the Duke of Austria[5], who imprisoned him in a *secret*[6] place. *According*[7] to *legend*[8], his friend Blondel[9] tried to find out where the king was. At first he had no *success*[10], but then he discovered the prisoner by singing under the window of a castle when Richard took up the refrain[11] of the song. Blondel could enter his king's cell in *triumph*[12] after an enormous sum of money had been paid for the release of the careless adventurer.

[1] [kruːˈseid] [2] [kæmˈpein]
[3] [ˈmistʃif]
[4] [ˌeidriˈætik]
[5] [ˈɔ(ː)striə]
[6] [ˈsiːkrət]
[7] [əˈkɔːdiŋ] [8] [ˈledʒənd]
[9] [ˈblʌndl, blɔnˈdel]
[10] [səkˈses]
[11] [riˈfrein]
[12] [ˈtraiʌmf]

Captain Scott

When Captain Scott and his brave *comrades*[1] started on their journey into the *immense*[2] desert[3] of the Antarctic[4] in 1911, they knew that the Norwegian[5] Amundsen[6], an *expert*[7] on the Arctic, was also trying to reach the Pole.
About three months later, they found the Norwegian flag close to the Pole. Amundsen had been *destined*[8] to be the first man at the South Pole. In spite of all their *efforts*[9] Scott and his men were over a month late.
On their march the British expedition had set up eight *depots*[10] with food for the return journey, which they began immediately. "We must face nine hundred miles of *solid*[11] dragging," Scott wrote in his diary.
The greatest *obstacles*[12] were the *constant*[13], *intense*[14] cold of more than forty degrees below zero and the continuous snowstorms.
One of the men *collapsed*[15] with *fatigue*[16] and died. Soon after another man was unable to march any further and met his death in the blizzard.
Some days later neither Scott nor the other two men were able to walk on against the storm *although*[17] they were only a few miles from the next *depot*[10]. Their bodies were found in their snow-covered tent eight months later. Thus one of the greatest achievements in the history of *mankind*[18] had come to a tragic end.

[1] [ˈkɔmr(e)id(z), *Am.* ~ræd(z)] [2] [iˈmens]
[3] [ˈdezət] [4] [ænˈtɑːktik]
[5] [nɔːˈwiːdʒən]
[6] [ˈɑːmundsən] [7] [ˈekspəːt]
[8] [ˈdestin(d)]
[9] [ˈefət]
[10] [ˈdepəu(z), *Am.* ˈdiː~]
[11] [ˈsɔlid]
[12] [ˈɔbstəkl(z)] [13] [ˈkɔnstənt]
[14] [inˈtens]
[15] [kəˈlæps(t)] [16] [fəˈtiːg]
[17] [ɔːlˈðəu]
[18] [mænˈkaind]

The Tramp

The tramp had spent a cold night on a bench in the park and he knew that he had to provide against the coming winter. It was an *absurd*[1] idea, of course, to dream of a big *hotel*[2] in Florida; three months in prison was all he was *interested*[3] in.
The pleasantest way to get there was to dine luxuriously[4] at some expensive restaurant. Having no money to pay for the meal, he would soon be handed over to the *police*[5]. As his *jacket*[6] was *decent*[7] and his *moustache*[8] was not too shaggy, he dared to enter

[1] [əbˈsəːd, ~ˈzəːd]
[2] [həuˈtel] [3] [ˈintrəstid]
[4] [ləgˈʒuəriəsli]
[5] [pəˈliːs] [6] [ˈdʒækit]
[7] [ˈdiːsnt] [8] [məˈstɑːʃ]

a fine restaurant, the only *access*[9] to which was through a big revolving door. [9]['ækses]
He would have succeeded in reaching a table if the headwaiter had not noticed his worn-out trousers. The waiter and two of his *colleagues*[10] carried him to a sidewalk without *disputing*[11] with him. [10]['kɔli:g(z)] [11][dis'pju:tiŋ]
After some other unsuccessful attempts to find *refuge*[12] from the cold winter, he stopped in front of an old church. The sound of the *organ*[13] could be heard in the street. Suddenly he felt that those *solemn*[14] notes were a great *comfort*[15] to him and had caused a *complete*[16] change in his soul. A strong *impulse*[17] moved him to *combat*[18] his desperate fate. He was still young, he could find a job, perhaps a *brilliant*[19] *career*[20] as an *artist*[21] lay ahead of him, he might even be in *Congress*[22] or become a *senator*[23]. [12]['refju:dʒ] [13]['ɔ:gən] [14]['sɔləm] [15]['kʌmfət] [16][kəm'pli:t] [17]['impʌls] [18]['kɔmbæt] [19]['briliənt] [20][kə'riə] [21]['ɑ:tist] [22]['kɔŋgres]
Suddenly he felt a hand on his arm. He turned round and looked at the bulky *figure*[24] of a policeman. "What are you doing here?" asked the officer. "That's no *concern*[25] of yours," answered the tramp. "Then come along with me," said the policeman. *(Based on: O. Henry, The Cop and the Anthem)* [23]['senətə] [24]['figə] [25][kən'sə:n]

2,3,4, 5,7

2. Words of Three and More Syllables: ´– – – or – ´– – or – – ´– ?

Read aloud (after you have read aloud the English words in §§ 2, 3–5 and 7 of HOW TO AVOID MISTAKES).

a) Similar Words

1. admiral – cathedral – interval – spiritual – immoral
   agitator – orator – spectator – ancestor – calendar
   architect – dialect – intellect – imperfect – to recollect
   article – vehicle – miracle
   benefit – to deposit – opposite – infinite – appetite
   gratitude – attitude – multitude
   Catholic – republic – arithmetic – politics
   avarice – prejudice – sacrifice
   cabinet – to interpret – violet
   catalogue – dialogue – monologue
   element – parliament – compliment – monument – accompaniment
2. discipline – to determine – to examine
   compromise – exercise
   analysis – emphasis
   literature – signature – temperature
   character – minister – register
   substitute – absolute – to constitute – to distribute
   Catholicism – Protestantism
   to abandon – companion – television – horizon
   refugee – committee
   uncertain – to ascertain – to entertain
3. tendency – constituency – intimacy – supremacy

accuracy – aristocracy – democracy – delicacy
agony – philosophy – academy – melancholy – testimony
adversary – elementary – parliamentary – dictionary – voluntary
monastery – laboratory – cemetery
desperate – certificate – to contemplate – to illustrate
apparent – president – beneficent – opponent – evident
tolerant – abundant – indignant – extravagant – lieutenant
nominative – accusative – subjunctive – imaginative – relative
imperative – demonstrative – negative – illustrative – superlative
admirable – impossible – lamentable – comparable
ridiculous – superfluous – unconscious – infamous – monotonous
diameter – speedometer – thermometer

b) Situational Practice

1. A *thermometer*[1] is an instrument for measuring *temperature*[2]. Special *thermometers*[1] of great *accuracy*[3] are used in *laboratories*[4].
2. The *ancestors*[5] of our *automobiles*[6], built by *pioneers*[7] such as Daimler and Benz, and other old *vehicles*[8] have found a place in *museums*[9] all over the world.
3. Every five years a General Election is held. Britain is then divided into *constituencies*[10], and the candidate who has got a simple majority over his *opponent*[11] will get the seat in Parliament.
4. The House of Lords consists of members of the *aristocracy*[12] and some bishops who are called Lords *Spiritual*[13]. In our century the Lords have lost a lot of their power, but they can still delay an *ordinary*[14] bill for one year (a finance[15] bill only for one month) before it is sent to the Queen for the Royal Assent. Once a year the Chamber is the place for an ancient *ceremony*[16], the Opening of Parliament by the Queen.
5. Proverbs: *Desperate*[17] diseases[18] need *desperate*[17] remedies. – Every man is the *architect*[19] of his own fortune. – *Misfortunes*[20] never come singly. – Two *negatives*[21] make an *affirmative*[22].
6. Efficiency[23] expert[24]: "You're wasting *entirely*[25] too much time on your personal appearance."
Stenographer[26]: "But it's not wasted; I've been here only six months and I'm already engaged to the junior partner."

[1] [θəˈmɔmitə] [2] [ˈtemprətʃə]
[3] [ˈækjərəsi]
[4] [ləˈbɔrətri(z), *Am.* ˈlæbrətɔri(z)]
[5] [ˈænsistə(z)]
[6] [ˈɔːtəməbiːl(z), *Am.* - - - ˊ]
[7] [ˌpaiəˈniə(z)] [8] [ˈviːikl(z)]
[9] [mjuːˈziəm(z)]
[10] [kənˈstitʃuənsi(z)]
[11] [əˈpəunənt]
[12] [ˌærisˈtɔkrəsi]
[13] [ˈspiritʃuəl]
[14] [ˈɔːdnri, *Am.* ~neri]
[15] [ˈfainæns]
[16] [ˈserəməni, *Am.* ~məuni]
[17] [ˈdesprət] [18] [diˈziːz]
[19] [ˈɑːkitekt]
[20] [misˈfɔːtʃən(z), ~tʃuːn(z)]
[21] [ˈnegətiv(z)]
[22] [əˈfəːmətiv]
[23] [əˈfiʃnsi] [24] [ˈekspəːt]
[25] [inˈtaiəli]
[26] [stəˈnɔgrəfə]

Speakers' Corner

Every weekend the *orators*[1] of Speakers' Corner attract the attention of crowds of people. Political *agitators*[2] as well as *conservative*[3] *patriots*[4] have complete freedom to express their *opposite*[5] opinions. Religious fanatics promise a terrible *catastrophe*[6], the end of the *universe*[7], with the only *alternative*[8] of starting a new and better religion. Amateur[9] healers *demonstrate*[10] the value of *vegetables*[11], *preferably*[12] *cucumbers*[13], for your health and sell pills with a *guarantee*[14] that they will cure everything. The most *ridiculous*[15] *ideas*[16] are put forward with greatest *enthusiasm*[17].

[1] [ˈɔrətə(z)] [2] [ˈædʒiteitə(z)]
[3] [kənˈsəːvətiv]
[4] [ˈpeitriət(s), *Am.* ˈpæ~]
[5] [ˈɔpəzit] [6] [kəˈtæstrəfi]
[7] [ˈjuːnivəːs] [8] [ɔːlˈtəːnətiv]
[9] [ˈæmətə(ː)] [10] [ˈdemənstreit]
[11] [ˈvedʒtəblz] [12] [ˈprefrəbli]
[13] [ˈkjuːkʌmbə(z)]
[14] [gærənˈtiː] [15] [riˈdikjuləs]
[16] [aiˈdiə(z)] [17] [inˈθjuːziæzm]

Companions[1] in *Misfortune*[2]

In an *interview*[3] a successful *architect*[4] and *engineer*[5] told about a funny *episode*[6] of his youth:
Once a friend of his, who was a trombone[7] player, asked him to take his place in the *orchestra*[8], though the *architect*[4] had never played the trombone in his life. "All you have to do is to imitate the other trombone player," said the friend.
The *architect*[4] had *already*[9] got through the greater part of the concert when the trombones suddenly had to play a solo. The two players blew their instruments with all their strength, but not a sound was to be heard. Both of them were *substitutes*[10].

1 [kəmˈpæniən]
2 [misˈfɔːtʃn, ~tʃuːn]
3 [ˈintəvjuː] 4 [ˈɑːkitekt]
5 [ˌendʒiˈniə] 6 [ˈepisəud]
7 [trɔmˈbəun] 8 [ˈɔːkistrə]
9 [ɔːlˈredi]
10 [ˈsʌbstitjuːt(s)]

Some Characteristics of the English Language

Whereas the Old English language had a full inflectional[1] system, even with the *subjunctive*[2] mood occupying a *prominent*[3] place in its grammar, Modern English has almost *entirely*[4] *abandoned*[5] all the *multitude*[6] of grammatical endings. With a few exceptions, e.g. the 's' of the third person singular of the present tense or *apostrophe*[7] + 's' for the possessive case, the old forms have either died out or become *superfluous*[8], owing to the growth of other and more efficient means of *indicating*[9] the relations of words in the sentence. The most *important*[10] of these means are a fixed word order and the use of prepositions and auxiliaries[11], above all the various forms of 'have', 'be' and 'do' ('do' not only in *negative*[12] and interrogative[13] sentences, but also in *affirmative*[14] sentences in order to lay special *emphasis*[15] on the tense or the sense of the verb).
The *tendency*[16] is always towards[17] greater simplicity. The *accusative*[18] of the interrogative[13] pronoun (whom), for instance, has given way to 'who' in colloquial speech and in time will follow other inflected forms into linguistic[19] oblivion[20]. Another interesting example is the slightly increasing use of analytical forms with 'more' and 'most' to express the *comparative*[21] and *superlative*[22] degrees of adjectives instead of synthetic[23] forms with '-er, -est'. "If it continues to *develop*[24] along its present lines, English will ultimately[25] have more in common with the uninflected languages of East Asia[26] than with the languages of Europe" (Orwell). The progressive reduction of the old inflexions, resulting in a great number of one-syllable words, gave the English language the *character*[27] of special shortness and conciseness[28], which is also due to the use of non-finites[29] such as the *infinitive*[30], the gerund[31] and the *participles*[32] instead of longer subordinate[33] clauses.
Owing to the standardizing influences of school, radio and *television*[34], regional[35] *dialects*[36] in Britain have tended to decline in recent years. Other factors that have *contributed*[37] to this development are the lack of *dialect*[36] *literature*[38] and the rush to the big cities together with the *subsequent*[39] urbanization[40] of life.

1 [inˈflekʃnl]
2 [səbˈdʒʌŋktiv]
3 [ˈprɔminənt]
4 [inˈtaiəli] 5 [əˈbændən(d)]
6 [ˈmʌltitjuːd]
7 [əˈpɔstrəfi]
8 [suːˈpəːfluəs]
9 [ˈindikeitiŋ]
10 [imˈpɔːtnt]
11 [ɔːgˈziliəri(z)]
12 [ˈnegətiv] 13 [intəˈrɔgətiv]
14 [əˈfəːmətiv]
15 [ˈemfəsis]
16 [ˈtendənsi]
17 [təˈwɔːdz, *Am.* tɔːrdz]
18 [əˈkjuːzətiv]
19 [liŋˈgwistik]
20 [əˈbliviən]
21 [kəmˈpærətiv]
22 [suːˈpəːlətiv]
23 [sinˈθetik]
24 [diˈveləp]
25 [ˈʌltimətli]
26 [ˈeiʃə, *Am.* ˈeiʒə]
27 [ˈkæriktə] 28 [kənˈsaisnis]
29 [ˌnɔnˈfainait(s)]
30 [inˈfinitiv] 31 [ˈdʒerənd]
32 [ˈpɑːtəs(i)pl(z)]
33 [səˈbɔːd(i)nət]
34 [ˈteliviʒn] 35 [ˈriːdʒənl]
36 [ˈdaiəlekt(s)]
37 [kənˈtribjuːt]
38 [ˈlitrətʃə]
39 [ˈsʌbsikwənt]
40 [ˌəːbənaiˈzeiʃn]

The Troubles in Northern[1] Ireland

What began in 1968 with demonstrations by Ulster's[2] half million *Catholics*[3] was not a religious quarrel but a new beginning of a *desperate*[4] fight for civil rights, better homes and jobs, and a voice in the *Protestant*[5]-dominated government of Northern Ireland. To understand the *atmosphere*[6] of hatred and the campaign of terror and blood – the *permanent*[7] bombing[8] and shooting in Belfast and the *massacre*[9] of Londonderry – it is *necessary*[10] to go back to the middle ages.

The series[11] of attempts to extend English *supremacy*[12] to Ireland began in the twelfth century; it was finally established during the Reformation when the Irish earls were defeated and a great deal of the best land in Northern Ireland was given to British *Protestant*[5] farmers together with certain *privileges*[13]. By 1700, Irish *Catholics*[3] owned only one seventh of the land and were totally excluded from *politics*[14] by a *Protestant*[5] *Parliament*[15] in Dublin, which was *abolished*[16] in 1800 when the whole of Ireland was incorporated into the United Kingdom.

Throughout the nineteenth century Irish *patriots*[17] fought for Home Rule, i.e. autonomy[18] under British sovereignty[19], strongly opposed by Irish *Protestants*[5] who were *determined*[20] to fight against it. The attempt to declare Ireland a *republic*[21] on Easter Monday 1916 failed and the leaders of the rebellion were *executed*[22].

In 1921 the island was divided into two parts, the Irish Free State and six *Protestant*[5] counties in the north as a part of the United Kingdom with its own *Parliament*[15] at Stormont. The partition, however, did not solve the problems; the illegal Irish Republican Army (IRA) began a long series of acts of violence with the aim of reunification of North and South.

When in 1949 the government in Dublin proclaimed the Irish Free State a *republic*[21] and *Parliament*[15] in Westminster passed the Ireland Act under which Ulster remained a British province[23] with its own *Parliament*[15], Northern Ireland had all the *elements*[24] of *parliamentary*[25] *democracy*[26], but was not at all democratic. Though one third of the population were *Catholics*[3], for years all twelve of the Northern Ireland *representatives*[27] in the British *Parliament*[15] were *Protestants*[5]. A graduation *certificate*[28] from a *Catholic*[3] school was enough to disqualify a man from a good job.

The IRA did not expect to win the war in *military*[29] terms; its strategy[30] was to make the crisis[31] so costly that England's *Conservative*[32] Prime *Minister*[33] Edward Heath and his *Cabinet*[34] would be forced into direct rule from London and caused to rethink their *attitudes*[35]. And, indeed, in March 1972 *Parliament*[15] in Westminster passed the Northern Ireland Bill, which suspended Stormont and its government for one year and gave the full *executive*[36] authority to a *Secretary*[37] of State for Northern Ireland.

As soon as possible a *compromise*[38] and a *recipe*[39] for reconciliation between the *adversaries*[40] without any *prejudice*[41] should be

[1]['nɔːðən] [2]['ʌlstə(z)]
[3]['kæθ(ə)lik(s)]
[4]['desprət]
[5]['prɔtistənt]
[6]['ætməsfiə]
[7]['pəːmənənt] [8]['bɔmiŋ]
[9]['mæsəkə]
[10]['nesəsri, *Am.* ~seri]
[11]['siəriːz] [12][sə'preməsi]
[13]['privlidʒ(iz)]
[14]['pɔlətiks] [15]['pɑːləmənt]
[16][ə'bɔliʃt]
[17]['peitriət(s), *Am.* 'pæ~]
[18][ɔː'tɔnəmi] [19]['sɔvrənti]
[20][di'təːmin(d)]
[21][ri'pʌblik]
[22]['eksikjuːt(id)]
[23]['prɔvins]
[24]['eləmənt(s)]
[25][ˌpɑːlə'mentri]
[26][di'mɔkrəsi]
[27][ˌrepri'zentətiv(z)]
[28][sə'tifikət]
[29]['militri, *Am.* ~teri]
[30]['strætədʒi] [31]['kraisis]
[32][kən'səːvətiv]
[33]['ministə] [34]['kæbinət]
[35]['ætitjuːd(z)]
[36][ig'zekjutiv]
[37]['sekrətri, *Am.* ~teri]
[38]['kɔmprəmaiz] [39]['resəpi]
[40]['ædvəsəri, *Am.* ~seri]

found, a way to pacify Ireland and to put an end to *sacrificing*[42] the lives of Ulstermen and to *casualties*[43] among the members of the Ulster Defence *Regiment*[44]. Mr Heath said that the decisions of his government had "opened the way for *representatives*[27] of the minority[45] to play a constructive part in the life of the province."

[41] ['predʒədis]
[42] [''sækrifaisiŋ]
[43] ['kæʒuəlti(z)]
[44] ['redʒiment]
[45] [mai'nɔrəti]

8 3. Words of Two Syllables (Homographs): ´– or –´ ?

Read aloud (after you have read aloud the English words in § 8 of HOW TO AVOID MISTAKES).

1. *Abstract*[1] nouns have less precise[2] meanings than concrete[3] ones, and therefore should be avoided as far as possible. — [1] ['æbstrækt] [2] [pri'sais] [3] ['kɔŋkri:t]
2. The stranger spoke English with a foreign *accent*[4]. — [4] ['æksnt, *Am.* 'æksent]
3. In chemistry a *compound*[5] is a substance consisting of chemically united elements. — [5] ['kɔmpaund]
4. The workers were not satisfied with the Trade Union's *conduct*[6] of their *conflict*[7] with the employers. — [6] ['kɔndʌkt] [7] ['kɔnflikt]
5. The company made a *contract*[8] with the town to finish the bridge by the end of the year. — [8] ['kɔntrækt]
6. In construction and workmanship the new building *contrasts*[9] badly with the older ones. — [9] [kən'trɑ:st(s)]
7. The tramp was *convicted*[10] of theft. — [10] [kən'vikt(id)]
8. Haven't you got an *increase*[11] in salary this year? — [11] ['inkri:s]
9. He *deserted*[12] his family and travelled round the world. For some months he worked in an oil field in the Sahara *Desert*[13]. — [12] [di'zə:t(id)] [13] ['dezət]
10. Reader's *Digest*[14] is a well-known American magazine. — [14] ['daidʒest]
11. The prisoners were taken under *escort*[15] to another prison. — [15] ['eskɔ:t]
12. Canada's *exports*[16] of wheat are remarkable. — [16] ['ekspɔ:t(s)]
13. Part of the inland *transport*[17] system in Britain was nationalized, e.g. British Railways and London *Transport*[17]. — [17] ['trɑ:nspɔ:t, 'træns~]
14. Some parts of the Riviera are much *frequented*[18] by Englishmen. — [18] [fri:'kwent(id)]
15. The gentleman swallowed[19] the *insult*[20] without showing any emotion. — [19] ['swɔləu(d)] [20] ['insʌlt]
16. The *project*[21] to build a tunnel[22] between Britain and the Continent has been discussed for years. — [21] ['prɔdʒekt] [22] ['tʌnl]
17. There was no admission without a special *permit*[23]. — [23] ['pə:mit]
18. I hope you are *progressing*[24] with your knowledge of English. — [24] [prə'gresiŋ]
19. Gandhi organized hunger strikes among the Indians as a *protest*[25] against racial prejudice[26]. — [25] ['prəutest] [26] ['predʒədis]
20. It is a disgrace that some people throw away *refuse*[27] wherever they like. — [27] ['refju:s]
21. From this tower you can *survey*[28] the whole town. — [28] [sə'vei]
22. In many countries political *suspects*[29] are kept in prison. — [29] ['sʌspekt(s)]

4. Different Stress in Cognate Words

9

Read aloud (after you have read aloud the English words in § 9 of HOW TO AVOID MISTAKES).

a) Cognate Words

1. democracy – democratic – democrat
   economy – economic – economical
   photography – photographic – photographer
   industry – industrious – industrial
   ceremony – ceremonious – ceremonial
   origin – originality – original
   injury – injurious – to injure
2. to compare – comparable – comparative – comparison
   to compete – competent – competitive – competitor
   to alternate – alternate – alternative – alternation
   to demonstrate – demonstration – demonstrative
   to execute – execution – executive
   to administer – administration – administrative – administrator
   to legislate – legislation – legislative – legislature – legislator
   to prefer – preference – preferable
   to ignore – ignorance – ignorant
   to excel – excellence – excellent
3. courage – courageous
   advantage – advantageous
   atom – atomic
   commerce – commercial
   envelope – to envelop
   advertisement – to advertise
   reference – to refer
   maintenance – to maintain
   sustenance – to sustain

b) Situational Practice

British Industry

During the second half of the nineteenth century British *industrial*[1] and *commercial*[2] expansion[3] had a clear lead over that of other countries. About 1900, growing *industrial*[1] *competition*[4] from Europe and North America began to make itself felt. The new problems confronting British *industry*[5] and *economy*[6] in the twentieth century became apparent[7] after World War I. Goods from Japan[8], where labour was cheaper, established themselves in the large eastern markets, and coal from the newer European mines *competed*[9] with British coal.
After enormous losses of British capital during World War II, the government had to face another series of *economic*[10] problems in more recent years; it had to fight against unemployment and inflation and to try to *maintain*[11] *economic*[10] growth.

[1] [in'dʌstriəl]
[2] [kə'mə:ʃl]
[3] [ik'spænʃn]
[4] [ˌkɔmpə'tiʃn]
[5] ['indəstri] [6] [i'kɔnəmi]
[7] [ə'pær(ə)nt]
[8] [dʒə'pæn]
[9] [kəm'pi:t(id)]
[10] [ˌikə'nɔmik]
[11] [mein'tein]

Legislation[1]

The supreme[2] *legislative*[3] authority in the United Kingdom is the 'Queen in Parliament', that is to say, the Queen and the two Houses of Parliament. The Parliament at Westminster can *legislate*[4] for the United Kingdom as a whole or any of the constituent[5] countries separately[6]. It can also *legislate*[4] for the Channel Islands and the Isle of Man, but in these islands and in Northern[7] Ireland it is not the only *legislature*[8], for the Northern Ireland Parliament and the ancient *legislatures*[8] of the islands have power to *legislate*[4] on domestic matters.

Legislation[1] can originate[9] in either House with the exception of financial[10] bills, which are always introduced in the Commons. As a rule, however, bills likely to raise political controversy[11] go through the Commons before the Lords.

The system of delegated *legislation*[1], which is used to relieve pressure on parliamentary[12] time, empowers ministers to regulate *administrative*[13] details[14] after a bill has become an Act. In order to minimize the risk that powers thus *conferred*[15] on the *executive*[16] might weaken parliamentary[12] government, they are normally delegated to ministers of the crown, who are directly responsible to Parliament.

(Adapted from: Britain, An Official Handbook, 1967)

[1] [ˌledʒisˈleiʃn]
[2] [səˈpriːm] [3] [ˈledʒislətiv, *Am.* ~leitiv]
[4] [ˈledʒisleit]
[5] [kənˈstitʃuənt] [6] [ˈseprət(li)]
[7] [ˈnɔːðən]
[8] [ˈledʒisleitʃə]
[9] [əˈridʒineit]
[10] [ˌfaiˈnænʃl]
[11] [ˈkɔntrəvəːsi]
[12] [ˌpɑːləˈmentri]
[13] [ədˈministrətiv, *Am.* ~streitiv]
[14] [ˈdiːteil(z), *Am.* -ˊ]
[15] [kənˈfəː(d)]
[16] [igˈzekjutiv]

From the Constitution of The United States:

All *legislative*[1] powers herein granted shall be vested in a Congress of the United States, which shall consist of a Senate[2] and House of Representatives[3].

The House of Representatives[3] shall be composed of members chosen every second year by the people of the several States.

The Senate[2] of the United States shall be composed of two Senators[4] from each State, chosen by the *legislature*[5] thereof, for six years.

The *executive*[6] power shall be vested in a President of the United States of America. He shall hold his office during the term of four years.

The judicial[7] power of the United States shall be vested in one Supreme Court and in such inferior Courts as the Congress may from time to time ordain and establish.

[1] [ˈledʒislətiv]
[2] [ˈsenət]
[3] [ˌrepriˈzentətiv(z)]
[4] [ˈsenətə(z)]
[5] [ˈledʒisleitʃə]
[6] [igˈzekjutiv]
[7] [dʒuːˈdiʃl]

A Comparison[1] of Constitutions

Is it possible to *compare*[2] the American and the British Constitutions? Are there any *comparable*[3] institutions? Only in *ignorance*[4] can we try to make a *comparison*[1] between the Senate and the House of Lords, whereas the House of Representatives[5] and the House of Commons are *comparatively*[6] similar in *political*[7] power and functions.

The main difference between the British and the American Constitutions is the clear division between the *Executive*[8] and the *Legislative*[9]. This separation of powers is of *historical*[10] *origin*[11], for in

[1] [kəmˈpærisn] [2] [kəmˈpɛə]
[3] [ˈkɔmprəbl] [4] [ˈignərəns]
[5] [ˌrepriˈzentətiv(z)]
[6] [kəmˈpærətivli]
[7] [pəˈlitikl]
[8] [igˈzekjutiv]
[9] [ˈledʒislətiv, *Am.* ~leitiv]

the eighteenth century British colonies were *administered*[12] by a governor who was not responsible to the *legislature*[13]. This situation gives the American President certain *advantages*[14] over the British Prime Minister because he cannot be controlled by Congress. On the other hand, the Prime Minister is in a more *advantageous*[15] position because he can rely on a majority in Parliament, whereas in the United States there can be complete disharmony between a Republican President, for example, and a *Democratic*[16] majority in Congress.

[10] [hiˈstɔrikl]
[11] [ˈɔrədʒin]
[12] [ədˈministə]
[13] [ˈledʒisleitʃə]
[14] [ədˈvɑːntidʒ(iz)]
[15] [ˌædvənˈteidʒəs]
[16] [ˌdeməˈkrætik]

1,2,3, 6,9

Patients, Public and Private[1]

The National[2] Health Service has been in existence now for nearly a quarter of a century, but *private*[1] practice continues and seems likely to remain a *permanent*[3] part of the British medical scene. So it should. To suppose that all patients[4] ever can be treated *absolutely*[5] equally in every respect is an illusion[6]. It would be *manifestly*[7] *absurd*[8] for a *Cabinet*[9] *Minister*[10] not to be able to have a minor operation at the time of his choice.
Some priorities are bound to be *determined*[11] on non-medical grounds. This could be done by purely *administrative*[12] decision, which would be invidious for the *administrators*[13] – where to draw the line between the *important*[14] and the *self-important*[14] patient[4] – and could open the way to petty corruption. Or it can be done by personal payment – paying for convenience – which is more open and more satisfactory in every way. So the practical question is not whether there should be a *private*[1] medical sector, but how large it should be. *(From THE TIMES, March 1972)*

[1] [ˈpraivit] [2] [ˈnæʃnl]
[3] [ˈpəːmənənt]
[4] [ˈpeiʃnt(s)]
[5] [ˈæbsəluːtli] [6] [iˈluːʒn]
[7] [ˈmænifestli] [8] [əbˈsəːd]
[9] [ˈkæbinət] [10] [ˈministə]
[11] [diˈtəːmin(d)]
[12] [ədˈministrətiv, *Am.* ~streitiv]
[13] [ədˈministreitə(z)]
[14] [imˈpɔːtnt]

B. Sounds and Their Spelling

1. Vowels and Diphthongs

10–29

a → [æ] [ɑː] [ei] [ɔː] [ɔ] [ə] [i] [ɛə] [əu]

§§ **13** **14** **25** **16** 15 21 11 (28) (27)
of HOW TO AVOID MISTAKES

a) Find the 'odd man out'.*

Read the words aloud. The §§ given above will help you.

[ɑː] 1. to grant, to pant, shan't, to slant
2. clasp, gasp, wasp, grasp
3. pasture, passport, moustache, trespass
[æ] 4. drastic, plastic, sarcastic, blast
5. rascal, ration, talent, cancer
6. anger, manger, gravel, panel
7. alas, brass, mass, masculine

* *based on British pronunciation*

[ei] 8. to maintain, to ascertain, maintenance, villain
9. base, case, vase, bass
10. caste, radar, patron, chaos
[ɔː] 11. bald, dwarf, altar, yacht
12. haughty, gauge, vault, naughty
13. aunt, to haunt, to launch, to applaud
[i] 14. preface, surface, boatrace, lettuce
[ɛə] 15. dairy, prayer, mayor, major

b) Situational Practice

Read aloud (after you have read aloud the English words with **a** *in the §§ given above).*

1. The excessive use of *plastic*[1] materials will be *fatal*[2] to our environment[3]. Burning them, the only way to destroy them, will result in greater air pollution.
[1][ˈplæstik] [2][ˈfeitl] [3][inˈvaiərnmənt]

2. The *masked*[4] burglar opened the drawer and *grasped*[5] the precious[6] *necklace*[7]; then he disappeared through the window. The only traces he left were some footprints in the *gravel*[8] of the garden walk, which were of little use in *ascertaining*[9] who he was. So there was only a *vague*[10] hope of getting the *necklace*[7] back if he tried to persuade someone to *purchase*[11] it.
[4][mɑːsk(t)] [5][grɑːsp(t)] [6][ˈpreʃəs] [7][ˈnekləs] [8][ˈgrævl] [9][ˌæsəˈtein] [10][veig] [11][ˈpəːtʃəs]

3. Major Appleby was a tall man with a *bald*[12] head, a small *moustache*[13] and a deep *bass*[14] voice; he died of *cancer*[15]. In an African war he and his *squadron*[16] had made a successful *assault*[17] on the enemy's main *base*[18].
[12][bɔːld] [13][məˈstɑːʃ] [14][beis] [15][ˈkænsə] [16][ˈskwɔdrən] [17][əˈsɔːlt] [18][beis]

4. The *yacht*[19] was still on the *quay*[20], ready to be *launched*[21]. The modern, *radar*[22]-equipped boat, which bore the name *FALCON*[23] in big *brass*[24] letters on its bow, had six *panelled*[25] cabins for the owner and his guests.
[19][jɔt] [20][kiː] [21][lɔːntʃ(t)] [22][ˈreidɑː] [23][ˈfɔːlkən, *Am.* ˈfæl~] [24][brɑːs] [25][ˈpænl(d)]

5. On returning from our *holiday*[26] abroad we had to show our *passports*[27] and to declare some bottles of *champagne*[28] and a beautiful *vase*[29] we had bought in Venice[30].
[26][ˈhɔlədi, *Am.* ~dei] [27][ˈpɑːspɔːt(s)] [28][ʃæmˈpein] [29][vɑːz, *Am.* veis] [30][ˈvenis]

6. An Act to amend the law relating to libel[31] and *slander*[32] and other malicious[33] falsehoods, called the Defamation[34] Act, was passed by Parliament in 1952.
[31][ˈlaibl] [32][ˈslɑːndə] [33][məˈliʃəs] [34][ˌdefəˈmeiʃn]

7. The *chancellor*[35] *cancelled*[36] the pensions[37] the *monarch*[38] had just *granted*[39] to some courtiers[40].
[35][ˈtʃɑːnslə] [36][ˈkænsl(d)] [37][ˈpenʃn(z)] [38][ˈmɔnək] [39][ˈgrɑːnt(id)] [40][ˈkɔːtiə(z)]

8. After drinking a large *quantity*[41] of *alcohol*[42] the old tramp *wandered*[43] about across the *pasture*[44]. Later he was found in the *swamp*[45] by a police sergeant[46].
[41][ˈkwɔntəti] [42][ˈælkəhɔl] [43][ˈwɔndə(d)] [44][ˈpɑːstʃə] [45][swɔmp] [46][ˈsɑːdʒənt]

9. A *chauffeur*[47] must be *capable*[48] of making some minor repairs to the *automobile*[49] himself.
[47][ˈʃəufə, *Am.* ʃəuˈfəː] [48][ˈkeipəbl] [49][ˈɔːtəməbiːl, *Am.* ~ˈbiːl]

10. The old lady was walking along the *promenade*[50] when a sudden *blast*[51] blew her hat off and swept it across the beach. *Gasping*[52] and *panting*[53] she ran after it and succeeded in catching it just before it rolled into the sea. Totally *exhausted*[54] she looked for a *vacant*[55] bench to take a rest.
[50][ˌprɔməˈnɑːd, *Am.* ~ˈneid] [51][blɑːst] [52][ˈgɑːsp(iŋ)] [53][ˈpænt(iŋ)] [54][igˈzɔːst(id)]

11. The audience *applauded*[56] the players of the *chamber*[57] concert for some minutes.

12. In the *preface*[58] to the guidebook you can read that it is *hazardous*[59] to walk *straight*[60] across a *glacier*[61] because of the crevasses[62] cracking the *surface*[63] of the gigantic[64] *mass*[65] of ice.
13. While you're eating those plums, look out for *wasps*[66]; it's dangerous to *swallow*[67] one.
14. Though similar in form, a *cradle*[68] and a *manger*[69] serve different purposes: a *cradle*[68] is a rocking bed for a baby, a *manger*[69] is a box for feeding horses or cattle.
15. Having lost their way in the desert[70], the men were forced to *ration*[71] the little water they had left. A few days later they came to an *oasis*[72] surrounded by some *palms*[73].
16. The standard *gauge*[74] of railways is 4ft. 8½in.
17. The *vault*[75] is *haunted*[76] by a great number of bats.
18. John is a *naughty*[77] boy, a little *rascal*[78].
19. They paid for their television set by *instalments*[79].
20. St Patrick is the *patron*[80] saint of Ireland.
21. Proverbs: A *dwarf*[81] on a giant's[82] shoulders sees more than the giant. – Make the best of a bad *bargain*[83]. – One *swallow*[84] does not make a summer.
22. One evening Mr Lee came home from his office in a very bad temper. "I'm going to give that new *chauffeur*[85] notice," he said to his wife. "That's twice he's nearly killed me." – "Oh, darling", replied his wife, "couldn't you give him another chance?"

[55] ['veikənt]
[56] [ə'plɔːd(id)] [57] ['tʃeimbə]
[58] ['prefis] [59] ['hæzədəs]
[60] [streit] [61] ['glæsiə, *Am.* 'gleiʃər]
[62] [kri'væs] [63] ['səːfis]
[64] [dʒai'gæntik] [65] [mæs]
[66] [wɔsp(s)] [67] ['swɔləu]
[68] ['kreidl] [69] ['meindʒə]
[70] ['dezət] [71] ['ræʃn]
[72] [əu'eisis] [73] [pɑːm(z)]
[74] [geidʒ]
[75] [vɔːlt] [76] ['hɔːnt(id)]
[77] ['nɔːti] [78] ['rɑːskl]
[79] [in'stɔːlmənt(s)]
[80] ['peitrən]
[81] [dwɔːf] [82] ['dʒaiənt]
[83] ['bɑːgin] [84] ['swɔləu]
[85] ['ʃəufə, *Am.* ʃəu'fəː]

c) Same Letter – Different Pronunciation

Divide the following words into groups according to their pronunciation and then read them aloud.

1. [ɑː] (§ 14) *or* [æ] (§ 13)?

alas, ant, blast, drastic, plastic, brass, mass, masculine, mask, to cancel, chancellor, cancer, clasp, grasp, sarcastic, rascal, hazard, grant, slant, to pant, slander, talent

2. [ɑː] (§ 14) *or* [ei] (§ 25)?

bass, base, vase, champagne, chaos, caste, oasis, radar, nasty, fragrant, plague, vague, pasture, simultaneous

3. [æ] (§ 13) *or* [ei] (§ 25)?

capable, chamber, panel, alien, ancient, fatal, ration, gravel, cradle, manger, anger, patent, patron, vacant, glacier, sacred, major, (he) bade, radiant

4. [ɑː] (§ 14) *or* [ə] (§ 21)?

passport, trespass, purchase, promenade, moustache, monarch, vinegar

5. [ɑː] (§ 14) *or* [ɔː] (§ 16)?

altar, alms, awe, awkward, bald, chalk, falcon, dwarf, halt, palm, instalment

6. [æ] (§ 13) *or* [ɔ] (§ 15)?

to swallow, squadron, yacht, wrath, equality, alphabet, swallow, swan, wallet, alcohol, to wander, wasp, quantity, swamp

7. **au** [ɑː] (§ 14) *or* [ɔː] (§ 16) *or* [?] (§ 25, § 27)?

draught, haughty, naughty, to exhaust, gauge, to applaud, applause, haunt, aunt, to launch, assault, vault, chauffeur, automobile, pause

8. **ai, ay** **ace** [i] (§ 11) *or* [ei] (§ 25) *or* [ɛə] (§ 28) *or* [?] (§ 21)?

bargain, to ascertain, villain, maintenance, fountain, to maintain, Monday, failure, dairy, mayor, holiday, preface, surface, straight, prayer *(thing)*

e → [e] [iː] [iə] [i] [ɛə] [juː] [əː] [ei] [ai] [əu] [uː] [ɑː]

§§ **12** **10** **29** 11 28 (19) (22) (25) (24) (27) (18) (14)
of HOW TO AVOID MISTAKES

a) Find the 'odd man out'.*

Read the words aloud. The §§ given above will help you.

[e] 1. lemon, to levy, lever, leopard
2. to sweat, to tread, to spread, to plead
[iː] 3. clean, to cheat, zealous, bead
4. species, precious, previous, prefix
5. ceremony, decent, veto, fever
6. heathen, creature, cheat, treachery
7. to seize, leisure, ceiling, to deceive
[ei] 8. freight, height, weight, sleigh
[ai] 9. kind, to indict, to kindle, viscount
[ɛə] 10. weary, pear, to swear, to bear
[iə] 11. gear, tear, to wear, dreary
[uː] 12. dew, view, to hew, to sew
[əː] 13. jerk, clerk, to determine, superb

b) Situational Practice

Read aloud (after you have read aloud the English words with **e** *in the §§ given above).*

1. The Clean Air Act of 1956 prohibited the burning of soft coal in *hearth*[1] grates in large *areas*[2] of Britain. British industry had to spend millions of pounds to clean up emissions from its *chimneys*[3].
2. She started the engine and put the *gear*[4] *lever*[5] into fourth *gear*[4]. The car moved a little and then stopped with a *jerk*[6]. The driving instructor said: "Miss Throttle, I'm sure you'll learn to drive a car; if you *persevere*[7] with it, you'll master it in less than a year."

[1] [hɑːθ] [2] [ˈɛəriə(z)]
[3] [ˈtʃimni(z)]
[4] [giə] [5] [ˈliːvə, *Am.* ˈlevər]
[6] [dʒəːk]
[7] [ˌpəːsiˈviə]

---

* *based on British pronunciation*

3. That box is as heavy as *lead*[8]. I have a weak *heart*[9] and cannot lift heavy *weights*[10].

[8][led] [9][hɑːt]
[10][weit(s)]

4. After the war a lot of people had to live in *refugee*[11] camps. They had lost their homes, and often the only things they owned were the clothes they wore. Sometimes they had not even a needle and *thread*[12] to *sew*[13] a button on.

[11][ˌrefju'dʒiː, *Am.* 're ~]
[12][θred] [13][səu]

5. An *alley*[14] is *either*[15] a narrow passage between buildings or a path in a garden or park.

[14]['æli] [15]['aiðə, *Am.* 'iː ~]

6. The news that a man-eating *leopard*[16] had killed a boy *spread*[17] quickly. About fifty villagers were soon gathered, among them the boy's father, who beat his *breast*[18] with his clenched fists while *tears*[19] of grief and wrath[20] were rolling down his cheeks into his rugged[21] *beard*[22]. The boy was still holding a stick in his hand, which he seemed to have used as a *weapon*[23] when the *leopard*[16] had begun to *tear*[24] his shoulder.

[16]['lepəd] [17][spred]
[18][brest]
[19][tiə(z)] [20][rɔθ, *Am.* ræθ]
[21]['rʌgid] [22][biəd]
[23]['wepən]
[24][tɛə]

7. The investiture[25] of Prince Charles as Prince of Wales at Caernarvon[26] Castle in July 1969 was a *medieval*[27] *ceremony*[28] of splendour and solemnity[29].

[25][in'vestitʃə]
[26][kə'nɑːvn] [27][ˌmedi'iːvl]
[28]['serəməni, *Am.* ~ məuni]

8. I can't *conceive*[30] why these children must always *tread*[31] on the flower beds. Early this morning – the grass was still wet with *dew*[32] – they were in the garden again. I *seized*[33] the opportunity and asked them to take greater care of the flowers – I could *swear*[34] that I was not brusque[35] to them – when their mother opened her kitchen window and told me not to *interfere*[36] in other people's affairs.

[29][sə'lemnəti] [30][kən'siːv]
[31][tred]
[32][djuː] [33][siːz(d)]
[34][swɛə]
[35][bruːsk]
[36][ˌintə'fiə]

9. Though it was some degrees below *zero*[37], his face was covered with *beads*[38] of *sweat*[39] while he was *hewing*[40] down the tree. It was an old *pear*[41] tree which did not *bear*[42] fruit any longer.

[37]['ziərəu]
[38][biːd(z)] [39][swet]
[40]['hjuːiŋ] [41][pɛə] [42][bɛə]

10. These Christmas trees were transported by *sleigh*[43] down from the *heights*[44] of the Rocky Mountains and then by *freight*[45] train to San Francisco.

[43][slei]
[44][hait(s)] [45][freit]

11. Proverbs: Keep your *breath*[46] to cool the broth. – Marry in haste, repent at *leisure*[47]. – *Neither*[48] great poverty nor great riches will hear reason. – *Discretion*[49] is the better part of valour.

[46][breθ] [47]['leʒə]
[48]['naiðə, *Am.* 'niː ~]
[49][di'skreʃn]

The *Peasants'*[1] Revolt (1381)

The reign of Richard II was an *epoch*[2] of great social tensions[3]. When an attempt was made to get money for a war by *levying*[4] a tax of one shilling (which was the wage of a skilled labourer for a week) on every adult head in England, the farmers around London *determined*[5] to rise up in arms. A *series*[6] of rebellions followed which became known as the *Peasants'*[1] Revolt.

[1]['pesnt(s)]
[2]['iːpɔk, *Am.* 'epək]
[3]['tenʃn(z)] [4]['levi(iŋ)]
[5][di'təːmin(d)] [6]['siəriːz]

Under the command of Wat Tiler[7] about 60,000 *peasants*[1] marched to London, burnt several houses and palaces of some great lords of the *realm*[8], and even *threatened*[9] to storm the Tower if the king did not come out to them. The king promised to grant them their wish: freedom from servitude[10] if they returned to their villages. The next day Wat Tiler was *treacherously*[11] taken and slain by some noblemen.

[7]['wɔt 'tailə]
[8][relm] [9][θretn(d)]
[10]['səːvitjuːd]
[11]['tretʃərəsli]

As Parliament put a *veto*[12] on the king's grants of liberty, the [12]['vi:təu]
peasants[1] never *received*[13] the promised charters of emancipation. [13][ri'si:v(d)]
They found that they had been *deceived*[14], but saw that they had [14][di'si:v(d)]
no hope of resisting any longer. They were not yet free, but still
legally[15] obliged[16] to do certain work for their lords. [15]['li:g(ə)li] [16][ə'blaidʒ(d)]
(Based on: Carrington-Jackson, A History of England)

The Black Sheep

Do you know my *nephews*[1] John and Bill? Bill is the black sheep of [1]['nevju:(z), *Am.* 'nef~]
the family; at least his brother John calls him that. John is an
engineer[2] and works for a big company. He is a *demon*[3] for work [2][ˌendʒi'niə] [3]['di:mən]
and *zealous*[4] to please his employer. Few of his *colleagues*[5] *equal*[6] [4]['zeləs][5]['kɔli:g(z)]
him in intelligence, and sometimes I think he is a mathematical [6]['i:kwl]
genius[7]. For his present position he had to *compete*[8] with two or [7]['dʒi:niəs] [8][kəm'pi:t]
three rivals[9]; it is a *key*[10] position which does not leave him any [9]['raivl(z)] [10][ki:]
time for hobbies or amusement and only little time for his
family.
Bill also began a *decent*[11] *career*[12]. He had been a *clerk*[13] with Aber- [11]['di:snt] [12][kə'riə]
crombie and Sons for three years when suddenly he was overcome [13][klɑ:k, *Am.* klə:rk]
by the *idea*[14] that working as an ordinary *employee*[15] was not [14][ai'diə] [15][ˌemplɔi'i:]
good for him. *Weary*[16] of working for "one pound an hour", as [16]['wiəri]
he said, he was *deaf*[17] to reason, and left London and went abroad. [17][def]
He was not at all *jealous*[18] of his brother's *career*[12]. [18]['dʒeləs]
When we next heard of him, he was a fruiterer[19] in Italy, dealing [19]['fru:tərə]
in *lemons*[20] and oranges. We were sorry to hear one day that he [20]['lemən(z)]
had *cheated*[21] somebody; of course, Bill *pleaded*[22] not guilty and [21]['tʃi:t(id)] [22]['pli:d(id)]
for some reason or other he really was not sent to prison. He
thought it best, however, to leave Italy and he *volunteered*[23] for [23][ˌvɔlən'tiə(d)]
the French *Foreign*[24] *Legion*[25] in Africa. A short time after he had [24]['fɔrin, ~rən]
been made a *sergeant*[26], he fell ill with a very dangerous *species*[27] [25]['li:dʒən] [26]['sɑ:dʒənt]
of tropical *fever*[28] and was allowed to return to London. [27]['spi:ʃi:z] [28]['fi:və]
Bill had not at all liked the *dreary*[29] life of a soldier, and after he [29]['driəri]
had recovered from his disease[30], he began to enjoy himself. When [30][di'zi:z]
he had spent the little money he had, he borrowed a tidy sum
from his friends, sometimes even from his brother John, who made
every *endeavour*[31] to get him back to work with the *heart*[32]-felt [31][in'devə] [32][hɑ:t]
promise that he would end in the gutter[33]. By the way, John was [33]['gʌtə]
much enraged when once he heard that Bill had bought some [34]['preʃəs] [35]['dʒu:(ə)l(z)]
precious[34] *jewels*[35] for one of his *pretty*[36] girls. [36]['priti]
The other day, on my way to my office, I met Bill. I was accustomed
to seeing him *wear*[37] *breeches*[38] early in the morning, because he [37][wεə] [38]['britʃiz]
used to go for a ride before *breakfast*[39]. Bill was in high spirits when [39]['brekfəst]
he told me that he had become engaged to an old woman who had
died the *previous*[40] night and had made him *heir*[41] to a large fortune, [40]['pri:viəs] [41][εə]
a yacht[42], a house in London and a house in the country with a [42][jɔt]
superb[43] *view*[44] of a lake. [43][su:'pə:b] [44][vju:]
I wonder what my other *nephew*[1] will say when he hears that.
(Based on: W.S. Maugham, The Ant and the Grasshopper)

c) Same Letter – Different Pronunciation

Divide the following words into groups according to their pronunciation and then read them aloud.

1. [iː] (§ 10) *or* [e] (§ 12)?

prefix, precious, previous, demon, decent, discretion, detail, epoch, equal, veto, species, series, to appreciate, medieval, genius, ceremony, to compete, fever, lever, to levy, legal, lemon, legion, leopard

2. [ɑː] (§ 14) *or* [əː] (§ 22) *or* [iə] (§ 29)?

to determine, to interfere, to persevere, jerk, clerk, superb, sincere, sergeant, dessert, zero

3. [(j)u(ː)] (§ 18, § 19) *or* [əu] (§ 27)

dew, nephew, to hew, to sew, view, review, jewel

4. **ea** [iː] (§ 10) *or* [e] (§ 12)?

breast, breath, heathen, tread, thread, bead, to spread, to plead, lead *(metal)*, realm, sweat, cheat, threat, to threaten, treachery, treacherous, weapon, colleague, zealous, jealous, cleanly *(adjective)*, cleanliness, creature, to endeavour, deaf, peasant

5. **ea** [ɑː] (§ 14) *or* [ɛə] (§ 28) *or* [iə] (§ 29)?

beard, heart, idea, dreary, hearth, to bear, gear, pear, to tear, tear, to swear, to wear, weary

6. **ee** [iː] (§ 10) *or* [i] (§ 11) *or* [iə] (§ 29)?

beer, career, breeches, employee, guarantee, engineer, volunteer, refugee

7. **ei, ey** [iː] (§ 10) *or* [i] (§ 11) *or* [e] (§ 12) *or* [ai] (§ 24) *or* [ei] (§ 25) *or* [ɛə] (§ 28)?

alley, chimney, heir, leisure, either, neither, freight, height, weight, to conceive, to deceive, to receive, key, ceiling, to seize, foreign, sovereign, sleigh

i → [ai] [iː] [i]

§§ **24** 10 11 of HOW TO AVOID MISTAKES

a) Find the 'odd man out'.*

Read the words aloud. The §§ given above will help you.

[ai] 1. divine, finite, to destine, pint
2. precise, treatise, franchise, missile
3. fibre, choir, idiom, item
[i] 4. wind, wilderness, to wind, vinegar
[iː] 5. maritime, magazine, marine, machine
6. niece, priest, mischief, to besiege

* *based on British pronunciation*

b) Situational Practice

Read aloud (after you have read aloud the English words with **i** *in the §§ given above).*

1. Television broadcasts of the conference were relayed all over the world by communication *satellites*[1]; most of them were *live*[2] broadcasts.
[1]['sætəlait(s)] [2][laiv]

2. Christians[3] are people who believe in Jesus *Christ*[4]; their religion is called Christianity[5].
[3]['kristʃən(z)] [4][kraist] [5][ˌkristi'ænəti]

3. Student: "I'm indebted[6] to you for all I know." – Professor: "Oh, don't mention such a *trifle*[7]."
[6][in'detid] [7]['traifl]

4. After a three-month *siege*[8], the inhabitants of the town, suffering from *famine*[9] and *fatigue*[10], had to *yield*[11] to the superior *technique*[12] and engines of the enemy.
[8][siːdʒ] [9]['fæmin] [10][fə'tiːg] [11][jiːld] [12][tek'niːk]

5. As his health was *fragile*[13], the old colonel[14] had been put on a *diet*[15]. Though he said that his *appetite*[16] was spoilt without it, he was not allowed to drink any alcohol[17]: no wine, not even a drop of *vinegar*[18], and only half a *pint*[19] of beer a day.
[13]['frædʒail] [14]['kəːnl] [15]['daiət] [16]['æpətait] [17]['ælkəhɔl] [18]['vinigə] [19][paint]

6. Letter to the Editor:
"Dear Sir,
Last year you printed an article, at least I think it was in your *magazine*[20], that interested me very much, but I have forgotten what it was. I lost my notes on the subject and cannot find the *magazine*[20]. Will you send me another copy of same, if it was your *magazine?*"
(From 'The American Observer')
[20][ˌmægə'ziːn, *Am.* 'mæ~]

7. One of the great *maritime*[21] powers, afraid of losing her *prestige*[22], brought together a *unique*[23] concentration of warships, among them several aircraft carriers and guided-*missile*[24] cruisers[25] and destroyers with 4,000 *marines*[26] on board.
[21]['mæritaim] [22][pre'stiːʒ] [23][juː'niːk] [24]['misail, *Am.* 'misl] [25]['kruːze(z)] [26][mə'riːn(z)]

8. By the First Parliamentary[27] Reform Act of 1832 the *franchise*[28] was conferred on the middle class. The succeeding Reform Acts extended the *franchise*[28] to workers in the towns, then to agricultural labourers and finally, in the twentieth century, also to women.
[27][ˌpɑːlə'mentri] [28]['fræntʃaiz]

9. Though English and German are *kindred*[29] languages which have a great deal in common, a German who *determines*[30] to learn English will be faced with several difficulties, such as the enormous vocabulary, the prepositional and other *idioms*[31] and the use of the non-*finite*[32] forms of the verb, the knowledge of which is of *vital*[33] necessity.
[29]['kindrəd] [30][di'təːmin(z)] [31]['idiəm(z)] [32][ˌnon'fainait] [33]['vaitl]

10. I can hardly believe that such a *trifle*[34] was *destined*[35] to make *mischief*[36] between the two brothers. Now they are not only *rivals*[37] in business, but each of them tries to *bias*[38] the opinions of their old friends against the other.
[34]['traifl] [35]['destin(d)] [36]['mistʃif] [37]['raivl(z)] [38]['baiəs]

11. In these *magazines*[39] you can find articles of all kinds: the latest *doctrines*[40] of *psychology*[41], a *treatise*[42] on education and *discipline*[43], descriptions of *machines*[44] in the *minutest*[45] details[46], *genuine*[47] *recipes*[48] for Indian food and pictures of *antique*[49] furniture[50].
[39][ˌmægə'ziːn(z), *Am.* 'mæ~] [40]['dɔktrin(z)] [41][sai'kɔlədʒi] [42]['triːtiz, *Am.* ~tis] [43]['disəplin] [44][mə'ʃiːn(z)] [45][mai'njuːt(ist)] [46]['diːteil(z), *Am.* -ˊ]

12. Proverbs: *Kindle*[51] a fire that you cannot extinguish[52]. – To

err is human, to forgive *divine*[53]. – Under water, *famine*[54]; under snow, bread. –

13. A father introduced his teenage daughter to a friend from his office. Throughout the introduction the girl did not say a word. Embarrassed, the father explained: "She's not used to talking until she hears the *dial*[55] tone."

[47]['dʒenjuin] [48]['resəpi]
[49][ˌæn'ti:k] [50]['fə:nitʃə]
[51]['kindl] [52][ik'stiŋgwiʃ]
[53][di'vain] [54]['fæmin]
[55]['dai(ə)l]

The Alibi[1]

The *priest*[2] had been murdered at 7 p.m. *precisely*[3]. He had just been *winding*[4] up a big old clock when a bullet[5] pierced first his neck and then the *dial*[6] of the clock and stopped it. His *niece*[7], who came half an hour later to do the kitchen for him, saw him lying on the floor and called the *police*[8]. Near the door the inspector found a *lilac*[9] *linen*[10] *handkerchief*[11] which belonged to a man who, of course, had an *alibi*[1]. He said he had sung in the *choir*[12] from 6.30 to 7.30. In spite of that he was *indicted*[13] for murder because the *police*[8] had found out that he had been in the church only during the first two *items*[14] of the programme. Then he had left the church quietly through a back door and killed the *priest*[2], who did not want to allow his *niece*[7] to marry him.

[1]['ælibai]
[2][pri:st] [3][pri'sais(li)]
[4]['waind(iŋ)] [5]['bulit]
[6]['dai(ə)l] [7][ni:s]
[8][pə'li:s]
[9]['lailək] [10]['linin]
[11]['hæŋkətʃif]
[12]['kwaiə]
[13][in'dait(id)]
[14]['aitəm(z)]

c) Same Letter – Different Pronunciation

Divide the following words into groups according to their pronunciation and then read them aloud.

1. [i] (§ 11) *or* [ai] (§ 24)?

precise, treatise, franchise, Christ, live *(adjective)*, pint, to wind, kindred, to kindle, bias, dial, vital, vinegar, rival, trifle, linen, lilac, finite, appetite, satellite, maritime, to destine, divine, to determine, to indict, to oblige, diet, diverse, to divert, item, idiom, choir, fibre, fragile, missile, horizon, wilderness, psychology, alibi, minute *(very small)*

2. [i] (§ 11) *or* [i:] (§ 10)?

niece, priest, mischief, to yield, siege, handkerchief; discipline, genuine, machine, doctrine, marine, magazine, famine, police, prestige, recipe, fatigue, antique, technique, unique

o	→	[ɔ]	[ʌ]	[au]	[əu]	[ɔ:]	[u]	[u:]	[ə]	[ə:]
		§§ **15**	**20**	**26**	**27**	16	17	18	21	22

of HOW TO AVOID MISTAKES

a) Find the 'odd man out'.*

Read the words aloud. The §§ given above will help you.

[ɔ] 1. colony, column, colonel, model
2. comedy, comfort, common, comment

---

* *based on British pronunciation*

3. focus, copy, posture, knowledge
4. cost, frost, revolt, to hover
5. concert, congress, conscience, constable
6. poverty, to worry, column, colony

[ʌ] 7. tongs, ton, tongue, onion
8. compass, common, to accompany, company
9. glove, oven, shovel, poverty
10. monkey, fishmonger, donkey, honey
11. touch, rough, trough, tough
12. cough, courage, cousin, to nourish

[əu] 13. hostess, hostel, gross, host
14. poll, toll, model, folk
15. process, product, progress, protest
16. to comb, potent, to postpone, despot
17. canoe, woe, mistletoe, toe
18. forecastle, odour, wound, opponent
19. goal, oar, cloak, foam
20. bowl, bow and arrow, brow, crow
21. to show, shower, snow, to grow

[au] 22. touch, couch, to crouch, to vouch
23. bough, plough, blouse, southern

[u] 24. bosom, wolf, worm, woman
25. brook, flood, hood, soot

[əː] 26. to scourge, to pour, journal, courtesy

b) Situational Practice

Read aloud (after you have read aloud the English words with **o** *in the §§ given above).*

1. As prices *soar*[1] again, the *cost*[2] of living will rise from month to month.
[1] [sɔː] [2] [kɔst]

2. If you want to see Scotland, you can easily hitchhike from one youth *hostel*[3] to the other. There are also excellent *coach*[4] services all over Scotland.
[3] [ˈhɔstl] [4] [kəutʃ]

3. When I opened the suitcase, I saw that I had left my dressing case at home. The *hostess*[5] was so kind as to give me a *comb*[6], a *sponge*[7], a bar of *soap*[8] and a razor.
[5] [ˈhəustis] [6] [kəum] [7] [spʌndʒ] [8] [səup]

4. People who *cough*[9] never go to the doctor; they go to the theatre.
[9] [kɔf, *Am.* kɔːf]

5. For the use of some bridges and roads a *toll*[10] has to be paid.
[10] [təul]

6. You should *postpone*[11] your *comment*[12] on the new *project*[13] until you have got a *copy*[14] of the chairman's speech.
[11] [pəˈspəun] [12] [ˈkɔment] [13] [ˈprɔdʒekt] [14] [ˈkɔpi]

7. Our football team could not score a single *goal*[15].
[15] [gəul]

8. She did not have the *courage*[16] to wait any longer among those old *tomb*stones[17] which *conjured*[18] up in her mind memories of the dead.
[16] [ˈkʌridʒ, *Am.* ˈkəː~] [17] [ˈtuːm~] [18] [ˈkʌndʒə(d)]

9. I'm sure he'll never break a *vow*[19]. I'm ready to *vouch*[20] for his honesty.
[19] [vau] [20] [vautʃ]

10. The hotel *lounge*[21] was poorly furnished with a *couch*[22] and some chairs. An old *journal*[23] lay on a small table with a thread-
[21] [laundʒ] [22] [kautʃ] [23] [ˈdʒəːnl]

bare[24] table*cloth*[25]. On the wall there were only some clothes *hooks*[26].

[24]['θredbεə] [25][klɔθ]
[26][huk(s)]

11. After the prince had ruled like a *despot*[27] for years, some *potent*[28] *opponents*[29] made a *revolt*[30] and took him prisoner.

[27]['despɔt] [28]['pəutnt]
[29][ə'pəunənt(s)]

12. The tiger *crouched*[31] behind some *low*[32] bushes[33] before it sprang at the zebra.

[30][ri'vəult] [31][krautʃ(t)]
[32][ləu] [33]['buʃ(iz)]

13. Not being *endowed*[34] with great talents[35], he has never *accomplished*[36] any task successfully. He has not even made any *progress*[37] in his *knowledge*[38] of bookkeeping. So I think that his employer had a clear *conscience*[39] when he dismissed him last week.

[34][in'dau(d)] [35]['tælənt(s)]
[36][ə'kɔmpliʃ, ə'kʌm ~]
[37]['prəugres, *Am.* 'prɔg ~]
[38]['nɔlidʒ] [39]['kɔnʃns]

14. The two sailors cast off the boat and *shoved*[40] it off from the shore in order to return to the steamer. They had already rowed half the distance when one of the *oars*[41] broke in the *foaming*[42] surf and the small boat overturned. Though some other sailors had watched the accident from the *forecastle*[43] of the steamer, they could not save their mates.

[40][ʃʌv(d)]
[41][ɔ:(z)] [42]['fəum(iŋ)]
[43]['fəuksl]

15. More than two thirds of the population of the United States speak the General American dialect[44]. The other two dialects[44], New England and *Southern*[45], are much more limited. The New England dialect[44] is nearer to British English in many respects. *Southern*[45] American differs from both General and New England American. It is characterized by a slow drawl[46]; many speakers lengthen stressed *vowels*[47], saying e.g. [jeis] or even [jeijəs] for 'yes'.

[44]['daiəlekt]
[45]['sʌðən]
[46][drɔ:l]
[47]['vau(ə)l(z)]

16. In the advertising *columns*[48] of British papers, especially in the so-called agony[49] *column* of the Times, people often and obviously with success appeal to the generosity[50] of their countrymen. They ask for money for various *purposes*[51], for furniture, clothes and other things, and even for old cars, sometimes a special *model*[52].

[48]['kɔləm(z)]
[49]['ægəni]
[50][ˌdʒenə'rɔsəti]
[51]['pə:pəs(iz)]
[52]['mɔdl]

17. *Poll*[53] means the procedure[54], the place and the outcome of the voting at an election. *Polling*[53] takes place at a number of *polling*[53] stations in each constituency[55]. The *poll*[53] lasts all day. The candidates who are successful at the *poll*[53] will be members of the House of *Commons*[56]. They are elected for five years, whereas the members of the US *Congress*[57] are elected for a term of two years (House of Representatives[58]) or six years (Senate[59]).

[53][pəul] [54][prə'si:dʒə]
[55][kən'stitʃuənsi]
[56]['kɔmənz]
[57]['kɔŋgres, *Am.* ~gris]
[58][ˌrepri'zentətiv(z)]
[59]['senət]

18. Last year we spent some days in a little cottage in the mountains, which looked like the home of Red Riding *Hood's*[60] grandma, with tall trees but – thank goodness – no *wolves*[61] around it. In the kitchen, whose ceiling was black with *soot*[62], there was only a small stove[63] for cooking; no *oven*[64] for baking bread or cake and no facility for grilling meat, which was often as *tough*[65] as leather. We had to fetch water from a *brook*[66] nearby.

[60][hud(z)]
[61]['wulvz]
[62][sut]
[63][stəuv] [64]['ʌvn]
[65][tʌf]
[66][bruk]

19. The Federation of Nigeria[67] is an independent republic within the *Commonwealth*[68]. Nigeria's principal exports[69] are *cocoa*[70] (200,000 *tons*[71] a year), groundnuts (800,000 *tons*[71]) and palm *products*[72] (kernels[73] and oil, 700,000 *tons*[71]).

[67][nai'dʒiəriə]
[68]['kɔmənwelθ]
[69]['ekspɔ:t] [70]['kəukəu]
[71][tʌn(z)] [72]['prɔdʌkt]

20. At Christmas English homes are decorated with holly and *mistletoe*[74] and sometimes also with paper chains and *balloons*[75]. The branch of *mistletoe*[74] hangs from the lamp in the sitting room and, if a *woman*[76] stands under it, she may be kissed. I remember

[73]['kə:nl(z)]
[74]['misltəu] [75][bə'lu:n(z)]
[76]['wumən]

a *courteous*[77] young *attorney*[78] who always *bowed*[79] to a girl before he kissed her.

77	[ˈkəːtiəs]
78	[əˈtəːni]
79	[bau(d)]

21. The rumours that our police *constable*[80], son of the local *fishmonger*[81], would marry the daughter of *Colonel*[82] Sir Reginald Hungerford spread like wildfire[83] through our *borough*[84]. They were only *nourished*[85] by attempts to smother[86] them. As a paper wrote about wedding preparations at Hungerford Manor[87], the rumours continued to *flourish*[88]. In the end everything turned out to be a farce or a *comedy*[89], at least as far as our policeman was concerned. On the other hand it was not *thoroughly*[90] 'much *ado*[91] about nothing', for Elizabeth Hungerford married a young Scottish nobleman a few weeks later.

80	[ˈkʌnstəbl, *Am.* ˈkɔn ~]
81	[ˈfiʃmʌŋgə]
82	[ˈkəːnl]
83	[ˈwaildfaiə]
84	[ˈbʌrə, *Am.* ˈbəːrəu]
85	[ˈnʌriʃ(t)]
86	[ˈsmʌðə]
87	[ˈmænə]
88	[ˈflʌriʃ]
89	[ˈkɔmədi]
90	[ˈθʌrəli]
91	[əˈduː]

22. Proverbs: Two's *company*[92], three's a crowd. – It is the early bird that catches the *worm*[93], – *Poverty*[94] is not a shame, but the being ashamed of it. – Love and a *cough*[95] cannot be hid. – It never rains but it *pours*[96]. – *Blood*[97] is thicker than water.

92	[kʌmpəni]
93	[wəːm]
94	[ˈpɔvəti]
95	[kɔf, *Am.* kɔːf]
96	[pɔː(z)]
97	[blʌd]

23. As black as *soot*[98] – as greedy as a *wolf*[99] – as innocent as a *dove*[100] – as hoarse as a *crow*[101] – as red as *blood*[102] – as tricky as a *monkey*[103] – as *tough*[104] as leather – as sweet as *honey*[105].

98	[sut]
99	[wulf]
100	[dʌv]
101	[krəu]
102	[blʌd]
103	[ˈmʌŋki]
104	[tʌf]
105	[ˈhʌni]

24. "Daddy, the teacher told us that we are descended from the *monkeys*[103]. – "*Nonsense*[106], perhaps you do, but I don't."

106	[ˈnɔnsns]

25. In England if you ask for more sugar, the *hostess*[107] fishes out a small extra lump. In Ireland the lady hands you the sugar *bowl*[108] to help yourself. In Scotland if you complain that your tea is not sweet enough, the good lady usually suggests that "Maybe you haven't stirred it".

107	[ˈhəustis]
108	[bəul]

Early Colonization in America

The first plans to found an English *colony*[1] in North America were made by Sir Walter Raleigh[2], one of the most brilliant[3] men at the court of Queen Elizabeth. He is said to have gained the favour of the Queen by spreading his *cloak*[4] over a muddy spot so that his *sovereign*[5] might walk across without soiling her *shoes*[6]. The Queen appointed him to several positions of trust and honour, and though his colonizing enterprises were not successful, his *efforts*[7] prepared the way for later colonists and the foundation of the Virginia *Company*[8] in London.

1	[ˈkɔləni]
2	[ˈrɔːli, ˈræli]
3	[ˈbriliənt]
4	[kləuk]
5	[ˈsɔvrin]
6	[ʃuː(z)]
7	[ˈefət(s)]
8	[ˈkʌmpəni]

The history of English settlement in America began in 1607 when three storm-beaten ships reached the *coast*[9] of Virginia and the surviving 105 men, among them the famous Captain John Smith – 49 of their *comrades*[10] had lost their lives during the *rough*[11] voyage – founded Jamestown. The settlers had a lot of trouble with the Indians, who 'crept on all fours from the hills, like bears, with their *bows*[12] in their mouths', as one of the men wrote.

9	[kəust]
10	[ˈkɔmr(e)id(z), *Am.* ~ræd(z)]
11	[rʌf]
12	[bəu(z)]

One day John Smith, who had loaded a *canoe*[13] with beads[14], bells and hatchets to trade these things to the Indians for corn, was attacked by the Indians and taken prisoner. He is said to have escaped being killed at once by showing the Indians his *compass*[15]. They looked in *wonder*[16] at the little needle that went around and

13	[kəˈnuː]
14	[biːd(z)]
15	[ˈkʌmpəs]
16	[ˈwʌndə]

tried to *touch*[17] it. Later on his life was saved by the intervention of the chief's daughter, who even helped the settlers with food like corn, beans and *onions*[18]. Smith governed the *colony*[1] for two years; then he was badly *wounded*[19] by an explosion of powder and had to sail back to England.

17 [tʌtʃ]
18 [ˈʌniən(z)]
19 [ˈwuːnd(id)]

After the second permanent[20] English settlement in America had been established in Massachusetts[21] by Puritan settlers in 1620, more and more immigrants came over from Europe and pushed the *frontier*[22], the borderline between cultivated land and wilderness, farther and farther towards the west in a *process*[23] which lasted for about three hundred years.

20 [ˈpəːmənənt]
21 [ˌmæsəˈtʃusits]
22 [ˈfrʌntiə, *Am.* frʌnˈtiər]
23 [ˈprəuses, *Am.* ˈprɔ ~]

It was not until the middle of the nineteenth century that a *company*[8] of pioneers[24] reached the valley of the Great Salt Lake, where they built huts for the first winter. When the *frost*[25] was out of the ground, they began to *plough*[26] and to plant corn. After some time the seed *sprouted*[27] and the danger of starvation seemed to be over. But then something terrible happened. One day *crowds*[28] of crickets swarmed over the fields to eat the tiny shoots. The people made fires, dug trenches, killed thousands with their *shovels*[29], they even *flooded*[30] the fields, but all in vain. The settlers were about to *lose*[31] all hope when suddenly a flock of seagulls from the lake settled on the fields and began to devour[32] the crickets in *dozens*[33], in thousands, in swarms[34] and thus saved the *colony*[1] from certain death.

24 [ˌpaiəˈniə(z)]
25 [frɔst]
26 [plau]
27 [ˈspraut(id)]
28 [kraud(z)]
29 [ˈʃʌvl(z)] 30 [ˈflʌd(id)]
31 [luːz]
32 [diˈvauə]
33 [ˈdʌzn(z)] 34 [swɔːm]

A Fine Sunday Afternoon

Last Sunday, friends of ours, who live in the country, visited us with their three children. After dinner the children said that they would like to go to the zoo. Though I had wanted to spend the afternoon in the *comfort*[1] of my home, listening to a *concert*[2] on the radio, I was destined[3] to *accompany*[4] them. I tried the mildest possible form of *protest*[5], "I *wonder*[6] if it will rain...", but the answers were "*Nonsense*"[7] and "Don't *worry*"[8].

1 [ˈkʌmfət] 2 [ˈkɔnsət]
3 [ˈdestin(d)] 4 [əˈkʌmpəni]
5 [ˈprəutest] 6 [ˈwʌndə]
7 [ˈnɔnsns]
8 [ˈwʌri, *Am.* ˈwəːri]

Then on our way to the zoo my car ran out of *petrol*[9], and I was just refuelling her with my spare tank when a sudden *shower*[10] came down. I tried to lock my anger in my *bosom*[11] when I saw the children smiling through the rear window.

9 [ˈpetr(ə)l] 10 [ˈʃauə]
11 [ˈbuzəm]

As I was the *host*[12], I had to pay for the tickets which *cost*[13] me more than a pound. Our country *cousins*[14] were not interested in *donkeys*[15] or zebras, in foxes or *wolves*[16], *owls*[17], parrots, *doves*[18] or *crows*[19], but only in lions, bears and *monkeys*[20].

12 [həust] 13 [kɔst]
14 [ˈkʌzn(z) 15 [ˈdɔŋki(z)]
16 [ˈwulvz] 17 [aul(z)]
18 [dʌv(z)] 19 [krəu(z)]
20 [ˈmʌŋki(z)]

First we went to the lion house. Tigers and lions are in bad *odour*[21] with me; I cannot stand their smell. In spite of that I had to stand in *front*[22] of the cage for half an hour because the children wanted to hear a lion *roar*[23]. Nothing, however, could *rouse*[24] the *drowsy*[25] animals; only one of the lions yawned[26] and *showed*[27] his big red *tongue*[28].

21 [ˈəudə]
22 [frʌnt]
23 [rɔː] 24 [rauz]
25 [ˈdrauzi] 26 [jɔːn(d)]
27 [ʃəu(d)] 28 [ˈtʌŋ]

We spent another hour with the *monkeys*[20] watching their *coarse*[29] tricks. One *stout*[30] *monkey*[20] – he had very thick *brows*[31] and seemed

29 [kɔːs]
30 [staut] 31 [brau(z)]

to *frown*[32] all the time – jumped down from a *bough*[33] of a tree and [32][fraun] [33][bau]
bounced[34] up and down on the back of one of his fellows, uttering [34][bauns(t)]
hoarse[35] shouts. Then suddenly he reached through the bars of the [35][hɔːs]
cage and tore off a little *brooch*[36] from the *blouse*[37] of my little [36][brəutʃ] [37][blauz, *Am.* s]
country friend, who began to cry her eyes out.
I was not in the *humour*[38] for seeing the bears; so we went home as [38]['hjuːmə]
soon as possible. At home I realized that I had lost my *gloves*[39] [39][glʌv(z)]
somewhere in the zoo.

c) Same Letter – Different Pronunciation

Divide the following words into groups according to their pronunciation and then read them aloud.

1. [ɔ] (§ 15) *or* [ʌ] (§ 20)?

colony, column, comedy, comfort, comment, company, to accompany, common, Commonwealth, compass, comrade, concert, to conjure, congress, conscience, constable, front, frontier, donkey, monkey, (fish)monger, honey, onion, sponge, ton, tongs, tongue, to wonder, borough, thorough, nonsense, worry, dove, glove, oven, to hover, shove, shovel, poverty, sovereign, dozen

2. [ɔ] (§ 15) *or* [əu] (§ 27)?

cloth, copy, comb, cost, folk, frost, gross, host, hostess, hostel, posture, poll, toll, model, cocoa, potent, process, product, progress, project, protest, to postpone, despot, opponent, knowledge, revolt, monologue, dialogue, catalogue, focus, forecastle, odour

3. [u] (§ 17) *or* [uː] (§ 18) *or* [ə] (§ 21) *or* [əː] (§ 22) *or* [əu] (§ 27)?

woe, worm, woman, wolf, colonel, tomb, canoe, toe, bosom, effort, ado, shoe, mistletoe, to lose, petrol, attorney, purpose

4. **oo** [u] (§ 17) *or* [uː] (§ 18) *or* [ʌ] (§ 20) *or* [?] (§ 27)?

brook, brooch, blood, hood, flood, loose, foot, soot, balloon, hook

5. **oa** [ɔː] (§ 16) *or* [əu] (§ 27)?

cloak, coarse, hoarse, coach, coast, oar, roar, foam, goal, soap, to soar

6. **ou** [ʌ] (§ 20) *or* [ə] (§ 21) *or* [əː] (§ 22) *or* [au] (§ 26) *or* [?] (§ 15, § 16, § 18)?

blouse, bough, plough, rough, tough, cough, trough, courage, cousin, to bounce, bounty, couch, touch, crouch, borough, thorough, courtesy, courteous, to pour, to flourish, to nourish, lounge, ounce, odour, to rouse, southern, humour, journal, scourge, sprout, stout, wound, to vouch

7. **ow** [au] (§ 26) *or* [əu] (§ 27)?

bow *(and arrow)*, to bow *(to bend the head or body)*, brow, bowl, to blow, crowd, drowsy, to show, shower, to endow, crow, to grow, gown, frown, owl, low, vow, vowel, snow

u → [u] [ʌ] [juː] [uː] [ə] [əː] [i] [e]

§§ **17** **20** **19** 18 21 (22) (11) (12)
of HOW TO AVOID MISTAKES

a) Find the 'odd man out'.

Read the words aloud. The §§ given above will help you.

[u] 1. bull, bullet, butler, butcher
2. tub, pulpit, pudding, to push
[uː] 3. fruit, suit, suicide, juice
[w] 4. to distinguish, biscuit, to extinguish, anguish
[ʌ] 5. furrier, cushion, duchess, lust
[ə] 6. mature, literature, to injure, temperature
[əː] 7. burglar, surgeon, to bury, to burn
[–] 8. vague, fatigue, colleague, ague

b) Situational Practice

Read aloud (after you have read aloud the English words with **u** *in the §§ given above).*

1. Do you think you can play that *tune*[1] on your *guitar*[2]?
[1] [tjuːn] [2] [giˈtɑː]
2. You have a *cushion*[3] on the sofa, and a pillow in your bed.
[3] [ˈkuʃn]
3. The ceremony of the Changing of the *Guard*[4] in front of Buckingham Palace is an everyday *occurrence*[5] – a favourite sight for London visitors.
[4] [gɑːd] [5] [əˈkʌr(ə)ns, *Am.* əˈkəː~]
4. On the Continent, if people are waiting at a bus stop, they loiter around in a seemingly *vague*[6] fashion. An Englishman, even if he is alone, forms an orderly *queue*[7] of one. (G. Mikes)
[6] [veig] [7] [kjuː]
5. She was suffering from *ague*[8] and a high *temperature*[9].
[8] [ˈeigjuː] [9] [ˈtemprətʃə]
6. Every morning he went by *tube*[10] from his home in a *suburb*[11] to his office; he was one of the many thousands of commuters.
[10] [tjuːb] [11] [ˈsʌbəːb]
7. The freedom of the press is one of the great *bulwarks*[12] of liberty and can only be restrained but by despotic governments. (Virginia Bill of Rights, 1776)
[12] [ˈbulwək(s)]
8. For dinner we had soup, meat and potatoes, *lettuce*[13] and *cucumber*[14] salad, wine, beer or orange *juice*[15], then Yorkshire *pudding*[16], some *fruit*[17] and coffee and *biscuits*[18].
[13] [ˈletis] [14] [ˈkjuːkʌmbə] [15] [dʒuːs] [16] [ˈpudiŋ] [17] [fruːt] [18] [ˈbiskit(s)]
9. The *League*[19] of Nations, which was formed in 1919, had its headquarters in Switzerland, one of the few *neutral*[20] nations in World War I.
[19] [liːg] [20] [ˈnjuːtrl]
10. During these five years a library of 20,000 volumes has been *accumulated*[21]; according to the *catalogue*[22] mostly German and English *literature*[23].
[21] [əˈkjuːmjuleit(id)] [22] [ˈkætəlɔg] [23] [ˈlitrətʃə]
11. I have just read in the *GUARDIAN*[24] that the fire on the *luxury*[25] liner was soon *extinguished*[26], so we can go on our round-the-world *cruise*[27] next month.
[24] [ˈgɑːdiən] [25] [ˈlʌkʃəri] [26] [ikˈstiŋgwiʃ(t)] [27] [kruːz]
12. There is no *arguing*[28] about his behaviour. His language is rather *vulgar*[29], and sometimes he behaves like a *bull*[30] in a china shop.
[28] [ˈɑːgjuiŋ] [29] [ˈvʌlgə] [30] [bul]
[31] [ˈmjuːtʃuəl]

13. Our *mutual*[31] friend committed *suicide*[32] in his bath*tub*[33] by connecting it with the electric *circuit*[34]. He was *buried*[35] yesterday.

[32]['s(j)uisaid] [33][tʌb] [34]['sə:kit] [35]['beri(d)]

14. The clergyman was not quite up to the mark that day and dropped with *fatigue*[36] after he had stood in the *pulpit*[37] for only little more than an hour.

[36][fə'ti:g] [37]['pulpit]

15. The policeman was seriously *injured*[38] in the *tumult*[39] of a fight against several robbers. His wife was in *anguish*[40] until she knew that the *surgeon*[41] had succeeded in removing the *bullet*[42] from his lungs.

[38]['indʒə(d)] [39]['tju:mʌlt] [40]['æŋgwiʃ] [41]['sə:dʒən] [42]['bulit]

16. Several famous men, among them Thomas Jefferson, Benjamin Franklin and John Adams put their *signature*[43] under "the *unanimous*[44] declaration of the thirteen United States of America" (Declaration of Independence, 1776), a *unique*[45] and epoch[46]-making document in the history of mankind[47].

[43]['signətʃə] [44][ju:'næniməs] [45][ju:'ni:k] [46]['i:pɔk, *Am.* 'epək] [47][ˌmæn'kaind]

17. Proverbs: Stolen *fruit*[48] is sweetest. – There's no *arguing*[49] about tastes. – *Virtue*[50] is its own reward.

[48][fru:t] [49]['ɑ:gjuiŋ] [50]['və:tʃu]

18. Two *burglars*[51] had broken into a clothing store and were *busy*[52] sorting out some *suits*[53] when one of them saw one marked $250. "Bill, look at the price of this one," he said, "that's downright robbery."

[51]['bə:glə(z)] [52]['bizi] [53][su:t(s)]

The Mink Coat

The *duchess*[1] had already wanted a new fur coat for weeks. Now she had sent for a *furrier*[2] and asked him to bring a collection of coats. When the *furrier*[2] came with his assistant, the *butler*[3] *guided*[4] the two to her dressing room. It was easy to find a coat that fitted the *duchess'*[1] slim *figure*[5]; one beautiful mink coat marvellously *suited*[6] her blond hair. She *hugged*[7] her husband when he paid more than a thousand *guineas*[8] for the coat.

[1]['dʌtʃis] [2]['fʌriə, *Am.* fə: ~] [3]['bʌtlə] [4]['gaid(id)] [5]['figə] [6]['su:t(id)] [7][hʌg(d)] [8]['gini(z)]

The next morning the *duchess*[1] missed her pearls. A detective found out that the *furrier*[2] and his *colleague*[9] had broken into the house during the night and had stolen the pearls and some jewellery[10]. They had been *burglars*[11] in the *disguise*[12] of honourable *businessmen*[13]. The duke easily recognized their faces in the *rogues'*[14] gallery. One of them was a real *furrier*[2], the other had been a *butcher*[15] by trade. By the way, the mink coat was only a good imitation; the *duchess*[1] had been unable to *distinguish*[16] it from a *genuine*[17] one.

[9]['kɔli:g] [10]['dʒu:(ə)lri] [11]['bə:glə(z)] [12][dis'gaiz] [13]['biznəsmən] [14][rəug(z)] [15]['butʃə] [16][di'stiŋgwiʃ] [17]['dʒenjuin]

c) Same Letter – Different Pronunciation

Divide the following words into groups according to their pronunciation and then read them aloud.

1. [u] (§ 17) *or* [ʌ] (§ 20)?

butcher, butler, bull, bullet, bulwark, duchess, furrier, cushion, to hug, lust, luxury, pudding, occurrence, pulpit, suburb, tub, to push, vulgar

2. [ju(:)] (§ 19) *or* [–] (§ 19) *or* [ə] (§ 21)?

pure, mature, figure, to injure, tumult, tube, nucleus, mutual, minute *(very small)*, cucumber,

queue, neutral, guarantee, guard, guardian, literature, signature, temperature, unanimous, unique, bugle, to accumulate, adieu, tune
league, colleague, ague, fatigue, rogue, vague, virtue, intrigue, plague, tongue, to argue, catalogue

3. [i] (§ 11) *or* [e] (§ 12) *or* [əː] (§ 22)?

burglar, to bury, busy, business, surgeon, lettuce

4. **ui** [uː] (§ 18) *or* [jui] (§ 19) *or* [w] (§ 19) *or* [–] (§ 19)?

suit, suicide, cruise, genuine, guinea, guitar, fruit, to distinguish, to extinguish, juice, guide, disguise, anguish

2. Consonants

30–38

g	→	[dʒ] [g]	**ng**	→	[ŋg] [ŋ]	**gh**	→	[f] [–]
		§ 30			**§ 31**			**§ 38**

of HOW TO AVOID MISTAKES

a) Find the 'odd man out'.

Read the words aloud. The §§ given above will help you.

[dʒ] 1. germ, gesture, gear, gem
2. legislation, eligible, allegiance, elegant
3. angel, anger, manger, to agitate
[ŋg] 4. longer, stronger, ginger, younger
5. angel, anger, angle, English
[f] 6. tough, through, trough, cough

b) Situational Practice

Read aloud (after you have read aloud the English words with **g** *in the §§ given above).*

1. Reader's *Digest*[1] is a well-known American magazine.
2. He is not good at *geography*[2]; he called Rotterdam the *Belgian*[3] and Copenhagen[4] the *Norwegian*[5] capital.
3. The standard *gauge*[6] for railways is 4ft. $8\frac{1}{2}$in.
4. A lot of diseases[7] are caused by bacteria and other *germs*[8].
5. I *suggest*[9] writing '*fragile*'[10] on the parcel as there is a china vase[11] in it.
6. *Vegetables*[12] are more easily *digested*[13] than meat.
7. The young lady was *elegantly*[14] dressed, but she made such an *exaggerated*[15] display of her jewels[16] that we had our doubts about their being *genuine*[17].
8. When – after a *gorgeous*[18] dinner – we were offered some drinks, my fourteen-year-old son said with an *ingenuous*[19] smile that he preferred *gin*[20] and tonic to *ginger*[21] ale.

[1] [ˈdaidʒest]
[2] [dʒiˈɔgrəfi] [3] [ˈbeldʒən]
[4] [kəupnˈheig(ə)n]
[5] [nɔːˈwiːdʒən] [6] [geidʒ]
[7] [diˈziːz(iz)] [8] [dʒəːm(z)]
[9] [səˈdʒest] [10] [ˈfrædʒail]
[11] [vɑːz, *Am.* veis]
[12] [ˈvedʒtəblz]
[13] [d(a)iˈdʒest(id)]
[14] [ˈeligəntli]
[15] [igˈzædʒəreit(id)]
[16] [dʒuː(ə)l(z)]
[17] [ˈdʒenjuin] [18] [ˈgɔːdʒəs]
[19] [inˈdʒenjuəs] [20] [dʒin]

9. The United Kingdom and her dominions were united by a common *allegiance*[22] to the crown.

[21]['dʒindʒə]
[22][ə'li:dʒəns]

10. The *surgeon*[23] was much *agitated*[24] about the death of his patient.

[23]['sə:dʒən] [24]['ædʒiteit(id)]

11. With *magic*[25] and *ingenuity*[26] the conjurer[27] produced five white *pigeons*[28] from his top hat.

[25]['mædʒik]
[26][ˌindʒi'nju:əti]
[27]['kʌndʒrə] [28]['pidʒin(z)]

12. I'd be much *obliged*[29] to you if you could have this letter *registered*[30].

[29][ə'blaidʒ(d)]
[30]['redʒistə(d)]

13. The main difference between the British and the American constitutions is the clear division between the Executive[31] and the *Legislative*[32]. This separation of powers is of historical *origin*[33], for in the eighteenth century British colonies were administered[34] by a governor who was not responsible to the *legislature*[35].

[31][ig'zekjutiv]
[32]['ledʒislətiv, *Am.* ~leitiv]
[33]['ɔrədʒin]
[34][əd'ministə(d)]
[35]['ledʒisleitʃə]

14. In Britain all men and women of eighteen years of age have the right to vote, except people who are subject to any *legal*[36] incapacity to vote, such as peers, aliens[37], persons of unsound mind and some sorts of criminals. The names of these persons therefore do not appear on the Electoral[38] *Register*[39]. With nearly the same exceptions anybody is *eligible*[40] to stand for election to the House of Commons.

[36]['li:gl] [37]['eiliən(z)]
[38][i'lektrl] [39]['redʒistə]
[40]['elidʒəbl]

The Two Castles

According to *legend*[1] the bigger of the two old castles on the mountain was built by a *giant*[2] who had a quarrel with a villainous[3] young knight. The *origin*[4] of the quarrel was that the knight carried away the *giant's*[2] beautiful wife when her husband was hunting in the forest; he found *refuge*[5] from his pursuer[6] in the smaller castle. Full of *anger*[7] the *giant*[2] laid *siege*[8] to it. Realizing after a few days that he alone could have no success, he went off and returned in the *disguise*[9] of a *beggar*[10]. The lord of the castle, a cunning and perfidious[11] man, allowed him to enter and had him thrown into a *dungeon*[12]. The *giant*[2], however, was strong enough to be able to break the door of the *dungeon*[12] and to set the castle on fire, but not until he had rescued his wife and carried some boxes full of gold and precious[13] *gems*[14] outside. At once he began to build another castle which was big enough for his *gigantic*[15] *figure*[16]. He *generously*[17] gave money to the poor in the country.

[1]['ledʒənd]
[2]['dʒaiənt] [3]['vilənəs]
[4]['ɔrədʒin]
[5]['refju:dʒ] [6][pə'sju:ə]
[7]['æŋgə] [8][si:dʒ]
[9][dis'gaiz] [10]['begə]
[11][pə'fidiəs]
[12]['dʌndʒən]
[13]['preʃəs] [14][dʒem(z)]
[15][dʒai'gæntik] [16]['figə]
[17]['dʒenərəsli]

*

15. *Hunger*[1] ist the best sauce.

[1]['hʌŋgə]

16. Full of *anger*[2] that there were not enough *hangers*[3] for his clothes, the famous *singer*[4] sent for the manager of the hotel.

[2]['æŋgə] [3]['hæŋə]
[4]['siŋə]

17. A Scotsman who comes to London may be a *stranger*[5] there. A German who comes to London is always a foreigner[6], even if he has been in England so often that he is no *longer*[7] a *stranger*[5] there.

[5]['streindʒə]
[6]['fɔrənə, 'fɔrinə]
[7]['lɔŋgə]

18. The first small group of English settlers who landed on that part of the coast found nothing but wilderness[8]. Having lost or used up all their provisions, they had to *angle*[9] for fish in the

[8]['wildənəs]
[9]['æŋgl]

nearby river to satisfy their *hunger*[10]. A great number of them died of starvation, only some *younger*[11] and *stronger*[12] men and women survived.

[10] ['hʌŋgə] [11] ['jʌŋgə] [12] ['strɔŋgə]

*

19. The old man burst into *laughter*[1] when his *daughter*[2] told him not to sit in a *draught*[3]. The next day he had *caught*[4] a most severe cold.

[1] ['lɑːftə] [2] ['dɔːtə] [3] [drɑːft] [4] [kɔːt]

20. *Though*[5] the sea was not too *rough*[6], it was a *tough*[7] job for him to sail the boat alone across the Atlantic. He had *enough*[8] time to think about his life in the past and in the future, and he often *thought*[9] of his family and his home in a small *borough*[10] in England while his boat was *ploughing*[11] its way *through*[12] the waves.

[5] [ðəu] [6] [rʌf] [7] [tʌf] [8] [i'nʌf] [9] [θɔːt] [10] ['bʌrə] [11] ['plau(iŋ)] [12] [θruː]

21. Love and a *cough*[13] cannot be hid.

[13] [kɔf, *Am.* kɔːf]

22. Diner: "Waiter, this is a very small steak!"
Waiter: "Yes, it is, sir."
Diner: "And on top of that, it's *tough*[7]."
Waiter: "Then I'd say you're lucky it's small."

c) Same Letter – Different Pronunciation

Divide the following words into groups according to their pronunciation and then read them aloud.

1. **g** [dʒ] (§ 30) *or* [g]?

gem, giant, guide, generous, genuine, gigantic, gesture, gin, game, genius, to get, ginger, geography, gallop, giraffe, gallery, germ
angel, anger, digest, to digest, disguise, gauge, league, to agitate, allegiance, ingenious, legend, eligible, elegant, dungeon, surgeon, bargain, pigeon, legislation, legal, magic, gorgeous, manger, margin, siege, refuge, origin, register, to forgive, to oblige, Belgian, beggar, to exaggerate, to suggest

2. **ng** [ŋg] (§ 31) *or not?*

anger, hanger, stranger, angle, angel, England, hunger, singer, English, longer, stronger, ginger, younger

3. **gh** [f] (§ 38) *or not?*

fought, enough, borough, tough, though, trough, through, thought, rough, plough, cough taught, draught, laughter, caught, daughter

ch → [k] [ʃ] [tʃ]

§§ **32** **33** **34** of HOW TO AVOID MISTAKES

a) Find the 'odd man out'.

Read the words aloud. The §§ given above will help you.

[k] 1. ache, anchor, archbishop, architect
2. champagne, chaos, chronic, chorus

3. mechanic, melancholy, orchard, orchestra

[ʃ] 4. chemist, chivalry, chauffeur, champagne

b) Situational Practice

Read aloud (after you have read aloud the English words with **ch** *in the §§ given above).*

1. Little Nellie complained, "Mother, I've got a *stomach-ache*[1]." "That's because your stomach is empty," her mother replied, "you'd feel better if you had something in it."
In the afternoon Aunt Annie came for tea and complained of a *headache*[2]. Little Nellie explained: "That's because your head is empty; you'd feel much better if you had something in it."

[1] [ˈstʌməkeik] [2] [ˈhedeik]

2. As our sewing *machine*[3] did not work, we sent for a *mechanic*[4].

[3] [məˈʃiːn] [4] [miˈkænik]

3. The strike left the rail service in a state of *chaos*[5]. Only the train from *Chicago*[6] arrived on *schedule*[7].

[5] [ˈkeiɔs] [6] [ʃiˈkɑːgəu] [7] [ˈʃedjuːl, *Am.* ˈskedʒ(u)l]

4. There is an *echo*[8] in the room; perhaps the sound is reflected from the *niche*[9] in the wall.

[8] [ˈekəu] [9] [nitʃ]

5. How long have you had your cough[10]? It's almost *chronic*[11], isn't it? You ought to go to a doctor or at least to the *chemist*'s[12] to get some tablets.

[10] [kɔf, *Am.* kɔːf] [11] [ˈkrɔnik] [12] [ˈkemist(s)]

6. It was a *melancholy*[13] sight for the old man to see that the storm had destroyed most of the trees in his *orchard*[14].

[13] [ˈmelənkəli, *Am.* ~kɔli] [14] [ˈɔːtʃəd]

7. Yes, you are right, that is Jane. She was a *chorus*[15] girl at the Royal Theatre. Then she married a famous *architect*[16], the one who developed a *scheme*[17] to rebuild our city centre. Now she has got a Bentley of her own; the young man with the *moustache*[18] is the *chauffeur*[19].

[15] [ˈkɔːrəs] [16] [ˈɑːkitekt] [17] [skiːm] [18] [məˈstɑːʃ] [19] [ˈʃəufə, *Am.* ʃəuˈfəː]

8. In May 1972 the 66,000-ton[20] 'Queen Elizabeth 2' was in mid-ocean when someone telephoned Cunard[21], her owners, and demanded a large sum of money in exchange for the information as to where the six bombs[22] were hidden aboard the Queen. Immediately after the call a team of four bomb disposal experts[23] boarded a long-range plane in Wiltshire, England. They came down by *parachute*[24] near the Queen a few hours later.
The passengers had no idea of what had happened; *orchestras*[25] played, *champagne*[26] corks popped and everything was as usual while the four men were searching the whole ship. No bomb[22] was found; the call had been a hoax[27].

[20] [tʌn] [21] [ˈkjuːnɑːd] [22] [bɔm(z)] [23] [ˈekspəːt(s)] [24] [ˈpærəʃuːt] [25] [ˈɔːkistrə(z)] [26] [ʃæmˈpein] [27] [həuks]

9. The reign of King Henry II was an *epoch*[28] of serious quarrel between the *monarch*[29] and the church. The cause of the quarrel was that Henry wanted the priests[30] to be tried by the royal courts whereas Thomas Becket, *Archbishop*[31] of Canterbury, did not want to have the churchmen brought under the control of the king.
As young men Henry and Thomas had been much *attached*[32] to each other, and Henry had even made Thomas his *chancellor*[33]. The quarrel ended in the murder of the *Archbishop*[31] by three of the king's knights, which really was no act of *chivalry*[34]. Becket was called St Thomas of Canterbury, and even the king, barefoot and in sackcloth, went on foot to Becket's *sepulchre*[35].

[28] [ˈipɔk, *Am.* ˈepək] [29] [ˈmɔnək] [30] [priːst(s)] [31] [ˌɑːtʃˈbiʃəp] [32] [əˈtætʃ(t)] [33] [ˈtʃɑːnslə] [34] [ˈtʃivlri] [35] [ˈseplkə]

c) Same Letter – Different Pronunciation

Divide the following words into groups according to their pronunciation and then read them aloud.

[k] (§ 32) *or* [ʃ] (§ 33) *or* [tʃ] (§ 34)?

archbishop, architect, (to) anchor, (to) ache, to attach, chaos, champagne, chauffeur, chemist, chorus, chronic, chivalry, Chicago, chancellor of the exchequer, echo, epoch, brooch, mischief, mechanic, machine, melancholy, moustache, monarch, niche, orchard, orchestra, parachute, scheme, schedule, scholar, stomach, technique

qu	→	[k] [kw]

§§ **32** **32** of HOW TO AVOID MISTAKES

a) Find the 'odd man out'.

Read the words aloud. The §§ given above will help you.

[k] 1. queue, to conquer, conquest, liquor
[kw] 2. banquet, liquor, liquid, conquest

b) Situational Practice

Read aloud (after you have read aloud the English words with **qu** *in the §§ given above).*

1. The Norman *Conquest*[1] began in September 1066, but it took Duke William several years to *conquer*[2] the whole of England.
2. Whisky, brandy, rum and gin are alcoholic *liquors*[3]. Water is a *liquid*[4].
3. The Prime Minister and the Chancellor[5] of the *Exchequer*[6] were present at the *banquet*[7].
4. In front of the church there was a long *queue*[8] of people who wanted to listen to a concert by the famous *choir*[9].

[1] [ˈkɔŋkwest]
[2] [ˈkɔŋkə]
[3] [ˈlikə(z)]
[4] [ˈlikwid]
[5] [ˈtʃɑːnslə] [6] [iksˈtʃekə]
[7] [ˈbæŋkwit]
[8] [kjuː]
[9] [ˈkwaiə]

c) Same Letter – Different Pronunciation

Divide the following words into groups according to their pronunciation and then read them aloud.

[k] (§ 32) *or* [kw] (§ 32)?

quay, queue, choir, conquest, to conquer, exchequer, liquid, liquor, antique, banquet, technique, unique

s → [s] [z] [ʃ]

§§ **35 36 33** of HOW TO AVOID MISTAKES

a) Find the 'odd man out'.

Read the words aloud. The §§ given above will help you.

[s] 1. such, suit, sugar, mason
2. to cease, to decease, to decrease, disease
[z] 3. paradise, dessert, dismal, husband
4. clumsy, jealousy, disaster, wisdom

b) Situational Practice

Read aloud (after you have read aloud the English words with **s** *in the §§ given above).*

1. *Research*[1] workers are still examining the question as to whether Milton wrote '*Paradise*[2] Lost' after his marriage[3] and '*Paradise*[2] Regained' after the death of his wife.
[1][riˈsəːtʃ, *Am.* ˈriːsəːtʃ] [2][ˈpærədais] [3][ˈmæridʒ]

2. The *deceased*[4] suffered from an incurable heart *disease*[5].
[4][diˈsis(t)] [5][diˈziːz]

3. There was an atmosphere of *tension*[6] when the prizes were given to the winners of the table-tennis match. Jane was third; she got a small silver cup that looked like a *sugar basin*[7].
[6][ˈtenʃn] [7][ˈʃugəˌbeisn]

4. He has a strong *aversion*[8] to brown clothes. I'm *sure*[9] he will never wear *such*[10] a *suit*[11].
[8][əˈvəːʃn, *Am.* ʒ] [9][ʃuə] [10][sʌtʃ] [11][suːt]

5. The word '*philosophy*'[12], derived[13] from two Greek words, means the love of *wisdom*[14] and knowledge.
[12][fiˈlɔsəfi] [13][diˈraiv(d)] [14][ˈwizdəm]

6. The old chauffeur[15] lives on a *pension*[16] in a small room under the roof of his employer's *mansion*[17]. As a young man he accompanied Lord S. on his travels through *Asia*[18], in *Russia*[19], *Persia*[20] and India.
[15][ˈʃəufə, *Am.* ʃəuˈfəː] [16][ˈpenʃn] [17][ˈmænʃn] [18][ˈeiʃə, *Am.* ˈeiʒə] [19][ˈrʌʃə] [20][ˈpəːʃə, *Am.* ˈpəːʒə]

7. The King James *Version*[21] of the Bible, which has had a sort of official status among English-speaking Protestants, was first *issued*[22] in 1611.
[21][ˈvəːʃn, *Am.* ˈvəːʒn] [22][ˈiʃuː(d)]

8. The chairman of the committee[23] laid special *emphasis*[24] on the fact that the population of several villages in the area had *decreased*[25] to a few hundred people, whereas there was a steady *increase*[26] in the population of the towns. He added that material for planning on a regional[27] *basis*[28] should be prepared, e.g. studies showing the economic[29] and social *resources*[30] of the area[31].
[23][kəˈmiti] [24][ˈemfəsis] [25][diˈkriːs(t)] [26][ˈinkriːs] [27][ˈriːdʒənl] [28][ˈbeisis] [29][ˌikəˈnɔmik] [30][riˈsɔːs(iz)] [31][ˈɛəriə]

9. On his return from the Third *Crusade*[32] King Richard met with *disaster*[33] in the Adriatic[34] in a storm which destroyed his ship. He got to shore and travelled by land across the Continent. In Austria[35] he was arrested and handed over to the German Emperor[36], who demanded an *immense*[37] *ransom*[38] for the *release*[39] of the king.
[32][kruːˈseid] [33][diˈzɑːstə] [34][ˌeidriˈætik] [35][ˈɔstriə, *Am.* ˈɔːstriə] [36][ˈempərə] [37][iˈmens] [38][ˈrænsəm] [39][riˈliːs]

10. After the factory had been in the *possession*[40] of their families for nearly seventy years, Watt and Smith *dissolved*[41] partnership. John Watt had proved a *false*[42] friend, and W. Smith could not be
[40][pəˈzeʃn] [41][diˈzɔlv(d)] [42][fɔːls]

absolved[43] from blame either. The factory buildings and the machinery are for sale now; it is possible that a big London company will *purchase*[44] them. So a famous old firm has *ceased*[45] to exist. 11. My niece's *husband*[46] is a strange example of the human *species*.[47] As far as I know he is a *mason*[48], who goes to work only on *Tuesday*[49], *Wednesday*[50] and *Thursday*[51]. He seems to live on *sausages*[52], for I have never *observed*[53] him eating anything else. He is as *clumsy*[54] as a bear, and his behaviour is sometimes *absolutely*[55] impossible, especially his *coarse*[56] jokes. I could tell you a *series*[57] of funny *episodes*[58] showing his extraordinary *curiosity*[59], which, however, is really nothing in *comparison*[60] with his *absurd*[61] *jealousy*[62]. The other day he attacked my niece with a pair of *scissors*[63] though nobody can live a more *desolate*[64] life than she. If things come to a *crisis*[65], he will have to be sent to a lunatic *asylum*[66].

[43] [əbˈzɔlv(d)]
[44] [ˈpəːtʃəs] [45] [siːs(t)]
[46] [ˈhʌzbənd] [47] [ˈspiːʃiːz]
[48] [ˈmeisn] [49] [ˈtjuːzdi]
[50] [ˈwenzdi] [51] [ˈθəːzdi]
[52] [ˈsɔsidʒ] [53] [əbˈsəːv(d)]
[54] [ˈklʌmzi] [55] [ˈæbsəluːt(li)]
[56] [kɔːs] [57] [ˈsiəriːz]
[58] [ˈepisəud(z)]
[59] [kjuəriˈɔsəti]
[60] [kəmˈpærisn]
[61] [əbˈsəːd] [62] [ˈdʒeləsi]
[63] [ˈsizəz] [64] [ˈdesələt]
[65] [ˈkraisis] [66] [əˈsailəm]

c) Same Letter – Different Pronunciation

Divide the following words into groups according to their pronunciation and then read them aloud.

1. [s] (§ 35) *or* [z] (§ 36)?

absolute, to absolve, base, basic, basin, husband, comparison, crisis, to cease, to decease, disease, to cleanse, to decrease, to increase, crusade, disaster, to dissolve, coarse, false, Thursday, dismal, emphasis, tense, paradise, to possess, immense, scissors, episode, precise, jealousy, clumsy, to observe, dessert, to prosecute, release, ransom, wisdom, sausage, species, research, resource, Tuesday, Wednesday, chase, purchase, philosophy

2. [ʃ] (§ 33) *or* [s] (§ 35)?

Asia, asylum, sugar, such, suit, sure, version, aversion, mansion, mason, compulsion, basin, Persia, Russia, sense, pension, tension, curiosity, issue

th → [ð] [θ]

§ **37** of HOW TO AVOID MISTAKES

a) Find the 'odd man out'.

Read the words aloud. The §§ given above will help you.

[θ] 1. north, northern, south, breath
2. birth, growth, smooth, tooth

b) Situational Practice

Read aloud (after you have read aloud the English words with **th** *in the §§ given above).*

1. With the presidential election of 1860 the differences between *North*[1] and *South*[2] became manifest[3]. In February 1861 eleven

[1] [nɔːθ] [2] [sauθ]

southern[4] states seceded[5] from the Union and formed the Confederate[6] States of America. The war that followed was won by the *northern*[7] states *with*[8] their superiority[9] in industry and manpower.

[3]['mænifest] [4]['sʌðən]
[5][si'si:d(id)] [6][kən'fedrət]
[7]['nɔ:ðən] [8][wið]
[9][səˌpiəri'ɔrəti]

2. He was *breathing*[10] hard, almost out of *breath*[11], after the race, but he had shown that he was *worthy*[12] of a place in the team.

[10]['bri:ðiŋ] [11][breθ]
[12]['wə:ði]

3. I don't want to take a hot *bath*[13] this morning. Let's go for a *bathe*[14] in the sea; it is quite *smooth*[15] now.

[13][bɑ:θ]
[14][beið] [15][smu:ð]

c) Same Letter – Different Pronunciation

Divide the following words into groups according to their pronunciation and then read them aloud.

[ð] (§ 37) *or* [θ]?

with, birth, to bathe, bath, breath, to breathe, growth, tooth, smooth, worthy, northern, north, south, southern

39 Silent Consonants

Read aloud (after you have read aloud the English words in § 39 of HOW TO AVOID MISTAKES).

1. At *Christmas*[1] English homes are decorated with holly and *mistletoe*[2].

[1]['krisməs]
[2]['misltəu]

2. Before World War I several American States had *prohibition*[3] laws, and a lot of US citizens[4] were *indicted*[5] for smuggling liquor[6].

[3]['prəui'biʃn] [4]['sitizn]
[5][in'dait(id)] [6]['likə]

3. Our former landlord was a gambler. When he had *exhausted*[7] all his savings, he ran into *debt*[8] and had to raise a *mortgage*[9] on his house.

[7][ig'zɔ:st(id)]
[8][det] [9]['mɔ:gidʒ]

4. An *exhibition*[10] of modern art has just been opened in the foyer of the *theatre*[11].

[10][ˌeksi'biʃn]
[11]['θiətə]

5. Soon after the successful landing operation the *corps*[12] was *softened*[13] up by heavy *bombing*[14]. The *wrecks*[15] of several landing craft and hundreds of destroyed land *vehicles*[16] of all sorts are still to be seen along the sandy beach of the *island*[17].

[12][kɔ:] [13]['sɔfn(d)]
[14]['bɔmiŋ] [15][rek(s)]
[16]['vi:ikl(z)]
[17]['ailənd]

6. Lord S. died of *pneumonia*[18]. At his funeral on *Wednesday*[19] only his family were present, among them his *heir*[20], the 13th *Viscount*[21] S., who put a large *wreath*[22] on his father's *tomb*[23]. Lord S. had been a man of *vehement*[24] character, whose most important *traits*[25] were courage and ambition.

[18][nju:'məuniə]
[19]['wenzdi] [20][ɛə]
[21]['vaikaunt] [22][ri:θ]
[23][tu:m] [24]['vi:əmənt]
[25][trei(z), treit(s)]

7. Before we began to *wrestle*[26], my opponent[27] *wrapped*[28] his *wristwatch*[29] into his *handkerchief*[30] and laid it on a bench. He was a tall and *handsome*[31] boy, and though he had long *limbs*[32] and strong *muscles*[33], I might have defeated him if my left *thumb*[34] had not begun to hurt with a *gnawing*[35] pain so that I could only grind[36] my teeth in helpless *wrath*[37].

[26]['resl] [27][ə'pəunənt]
[28][ræp(t)] [29]['ristwɔtʃ]
[30]['hæŋkətʃif]
[31]['hænsəm] [32][lim(z)]
[33]['mʌsl(z)] [34][θʌm]
[35]['nɔ:iŋ] [36][graind]
[37][rɔθ, *Am.* ræθ]

8. After *climbing*[38] for about seven hours, during which we had eaten all our *sandwiches*[39], we reached a small hut surrounded by

[38]['klaimiŋ]

an imposing Alpine[40] landscape[41]. Our hopes of finding some sort of restaurant or at least something eatable were destroyed. There was only an old *cupboard*[42] with some *crumbs*[43] of bread, two broken plates and an empty glass of *raspberry*[44] jam, but no *victuals*[45].

[39]['sænwidʒ, *Am.* ~witʃ] [40]['ælpain] [41]['læn(d)skeip] [42]['kʌbəd] [43][krʌm(z)] [44]['rɑːzbri, *Am.* 'ræzberi] [45]['vitlz]

9. It was already getting dark, and the *knight*[46] had not yet reached his castle. On his tired horse he was dreaming of a good meal near the fire when suddenly he heard something *rustle*[47] below some big *chestnut*[48] trees. Before he could *discern*[49] what it was, somebody *whistled*[50] and two *wretched*[51] *knaves*[52] ran on to the road from either side. They attacked him with their clubs and might have succeeded in *wringing*[53] his *sword*[54] out of his hand if he had not been on horseback.

[46][nait] [47]['rʌsl] [48]['tʃesnʌt] [49][di'səːn] [50]['wisl(d)] [51]['retʃid] [52][neiv(z)] [53]['riŋ(iŋ)] [54][sɔːd]

10. Proverbs: Death pays all *debts*[55]. – Hasty *climbers*[56] have sudden falls. – Red sky at night, *shepherd's*[57] delight; red sky in the morning, *shepherd's*[57] warning. – When in *doubt*[58], leave it out.

[55][det(s)] [56]['klaimə(z)] [57]['ʃepəd(z)] [58][daut]

11. Customer: "The turkey you sold me recently tasted abominable[59]." Grocer: "I can't understand that. It has received first prizes at *exhibitions*[60] for the last fifteen years."

[59][ə'bɔminəbl] [60][ˌeksi'biʃn(z)]

3. Different Pronunciation of Words of Similar Spelling

40

Read aloud (after you have read aloud the English words in § 40 of HOW TO AVOID MISTAKES):

1. He made every *effort*[1] to find a new and better home for his family. Soon he realized, however, that he could not *afford*[2] a house in one of the suburbs[3].

[1]['efət] [2][ə'fɔːd] [3]['sʌbəːb(z)]

2. Full of *anger*[4] the coach of the football team heard that one of his best players had hurt his *ankle*[5]. – The walls stand at right *angles*[6] to each other. – "And all the *angels*[7] in heaven shall sing on Christmas Day in the morning."

[4]['æŋgə] [5]['æŋkl] [6]['æŋgl(z)] [7]['eindʒl(z)]

3. Yesterday my *aunt*[8] found hundreds of small black *ants*[9] in her kitchen.

[8][ɑːnt] [9][ænt(s)]

4. Do you really believe that the ancient[10] Teutons[11] spent their lives lying on *bearskins*[12], drinking *beer*[13] and stroking their *beards*[14]? – These trees don't *bear*[15] fruit.

[10]['einʃnt] [11]['tjuːtn(z)] [12]['bɛəskin(z)] [13][biə] [14]['biəd(z)] [15][bɛə]

5. As her cook was ill, Lady M. sent her *butler*[16] to the *butcher's*[17].

[16]['bʌtlə] [17]['butʃə(z)]

6. The ship is on a safe *course*[18]; there is no *cause*[19] for anxiety[20].

[18][kɔːs] [19][kɔːz] [20][æŋ(g)'zaiəti]

7. As I was soaked[21] to the skin, I had to change my *clothes*[22]. – Northern[23] Ireland is the greatest linen producing region in the world; more than 50 million yards of *cloth*[24] are produced annually.

[21][səuk(d)] [22][kləuðz] [23]['nɔːðən] [24][klɔθ]

8. On Sunday we sailed along the *coast*[25] in John's new boat; it *cost*[26] him about £ 2,000.

[25][kəust] [26][kɔst]

9. In some regions of Germany it is still the *custom*[27] to wear traditional *costumes*[28] on Sundays. – Our luggage was checked by the *customs*[29] officials.

[27]['kʌstəm] [28]['kɔstʃuːm(z)] [29]['kʌstəm(z)]

10. The *deceased*[30] suffered from an incurable heart *disease*[31].

[30][di'siːs(t)] [31][di'ziːz]

11. A *monkey's*[32] *foot*[33] is like a man's *foot*[33]. – Meat is no *food*[34] for *donkeys*[35].
[32]['mʌŋki(z)] [33][fut] [34][fu:d] [35]['dɔŋki(z)]

12. The prisoners were allowed to play football in the yard of the *goal*[36] (jail). One of the teams scored two *goals*[37].
[36][dʒeil] [37][gəul(z)]

13. Water is a *liquid*[38]. Under high pressure and low temperature[39] air can be reduced to the *liquid*[38] state. – At our last party the majority of men preferred whisky to all other *liquors*[40] whereas the ladies had a special liking for some rather sweet *liqueur*[41].
[38]['likwid] [39]['temprətʃə] [40]['likə(z)] [41]['likjuə, *Am.* ~kə:]

14. "There is a nut *loose*[42] on your go-kart; don't *lose*[43] it." "Yes, I know; I had to *loosen*[44] it when I repaired a fault."
[42][lu:s] [43][lu:z] [44]['lu:sn]

15. The *mayor's*[45] daughter will marry *Major*[46] E.J. Bates in July.
[45][mɛə(z)] [46]['meidʒə]

16. The soldiers were on *patrol*[47] when they ran out of *petrol*[48].
[47][pə'trəul] [48]['petr(ə)l]

17. The Puritans desired a *pure*[49] form of worship. – Please *pour*[50] out another cup of tea for me. – We must help the *poor*[51].
[49][pjuə] [50][pɔ:] [51][puə]

18. Please go to the greengrocer's and fetch ten pounds of *potatoes*[52] and a pound of *tomatoes*[53].
[52][pə'teitəu(z)] [53][tə'mɑ:təu(z), *Am.* ~mei~]

19. The firm acknowledged the *receipt*[54] of the goods by return of post. – My mother has got a splendid new *recipe*[55] for a fruit cake.
[54][ri'si:t] [55]['resəpi]

20. There's no *soap*[56] in the bathroom. – Do you like *soup*[57] for lunch?
[56][səup] [57][su:p]

21. The workman wiped the *sweat*[58] from his forehead[59]. – Do you want your tea *sweet*[60]?
[58][swet] [59]['fɔrid] [60][swi:t]

22. The famous Mayflower was a vessel of 180 *tons*[61]. – In an angry *tone*[62] the master told the boy not to whistle the same *tune*[63] again and again.
[61][tʌn(z)] [62][təun] [63][tju:n]

23. The doctor asked me to put out my *tongue*[64]. – The blacksmith held the red-hot iron with a pair of *tongs*[65].
[64][tʌŋ] [65][tɔŋz]

24. I *wonder*[66] how long they *wandered*[67] about on the island before they found the hut.
[66]['wʌndə] [67]['wɔndə(d)]

41

4. Different Pronunciation of Cognate Words

Read aloud (after you have read aloud the English words in § 41 of HOW TO AVOID MISTAKES):

1. He was very *anxious*[1] about his mother's health. He waited with *anxiety*[2] for news of her operation.
[1]['æŋkʃəs] [2]['æŋ(g)zaiəti]

2. Joe has lived in *luxury*[3] all his life. He will spend the next three months in a *luxurious*[4] hotel in the Bahamas.
[3]['lʌkʃəri] [4][ləg'ʒuəriəs]

3. John is in the *bathroom*[5]; he is taking a *bath*[6]. – Take your *bathing*[7] costume; let's *bathe*[8] in the river.
[5]['bɑ:θru(:)m] [6][bɑ:θ] [7]['beiðiŋ] [8][beið]

4. The Queen *created*[9] him a *duke*[10]. – Isn't the young *duchess*[11] a lovely *creature*[12]?
[9][kri'eit(id)] [10][dju:k] [11]['dʌtʃis] [12]['kri:tʃə]

5. More than a hundred *nations*[13] took part in the Olympic Games in Munich[14]. A lot of sportsmen came to the opening ceremony in their *national*[15] costumes.
[13]['neiʃn(z)] [14]['mju:nik] [15]['næʃnl]

6. The accident was an unfortunate *occurrence*[16]; we hope that it will never *occur*[17] again.
[16][ə'kʌr(ə)ns, *Am.* ə'kə:~] [17][ə'kə:]

7. We greatly *appreciate*[18] your help in finding a good job for my
[18][ə'pri:ʃieit]

nephew[19]. – The duchess was wearing a necklace with some *precious*[20] jewels.

[19] [ˈnevjuː, *Am.* ˈnefjuː]
[20] [ˈpreʃəs]

8. He was *breathing*[21] hard after the race. He was almost out of *breath*[22].

[21] [ˈbriːðiŋ]
[22] [brəθ]

9. Mrs Jones is always *cleanly*[23] dressed; she is also said to be a *cleanly*[24] housewife. – My suit must be *cleaned*[25]. – You must try to *cleanse*[26] your heart of sin.

[23] [ˈkliːnli]
[24] [ˈklenli] [25] [kliːn(d)]
[26] [ˈklenz]

10. He has always shown *discreet*[27] behaviour. – *Discretion*[28] is the better part of valour[29].

[27] [diˈskriːt] [28] [diˈskreʃn]
[29] [ˈvælə]

11. The crew of the lifeboat were celebrated as *heroes*[30]. It was really an act of *heroism*[31] to rescue the shipwrecked people out of such a rough[32] sea.

[30] [ˈhiərəu(z)]
[31] [ˈherəuizm]
[32] [rʌf]

12. Mr Green is too *severe*[33] with his children; he often punishes them with great *severity*[34].

[33] [səˈviə]
[34] [səˈverəti]

13. With the Act of *Supremacy*[35] King Henry VIII made himself *supreme*[36] head of the Church of England.

[35] [səˈpreməsi]
[36] [səˈpriːm]

14. The North regarded the secession of the Confederate States as *treason*[37]. – You played a dirty and *treacherous*[38] trick on him.

[37] [ˈtriːzn]
[38] [ˈtretʃərəs]

15. Ted has been working with great *zeal*[39]. He always made *zealous*[40] efforts[41] to do his best.

[39] [ziːl]
[40] [ˈzeləs] [41] [ˈefət(s)]

16. After several priests had been hanged, a group of Roman Catholics *conspired*[42] against King James I and prepared to explode a charge beneath King, Lords and Commons in Parliament. One of the *conspirators*[43], however, warned his brother-in-law not to attend Parliament that day. Thus the *conspiracy*[44], which became known as the Gunpowder Plot (1605), was revealed.

[42] [kənˈspaiə(d)]
[43] [kənˈspirətə(z)]
[44] [kənˈspirəsi]

17. The witches *prophesied*[45] that Macbeth would be King of Scotland. Macbeth was rapt when he heard that *prophecy*[46].

[45] [ˈprɔfisai(d)]
[46] [ˈprɔfisi]

18. Macbeth was a cruel and unjust ruler, a real *tyrant*[47]. The whole country suffered from his *tyranny*[48].

[47] [ˈtaiər(ə)nt]
[48] [ˈtirəni]

19. The explorers passed through vast tracts of *wilderness*[49], full of *wild*[50] animals.

[49] [ˈwildənəs]
[50] [waild]

20. Do you *advocate*[51] the release of the prisoners? – Mrs Jones is a zealous[40] *advocate*[52] of equal pay for men and women.

[51] [ˈædvəkeit]
[52] [ˈædvəkət]

21. It was a *deliberate*[53] decision taken after hours of discussion. – They *deliberated*[54] where to spend their holidays.

[53] [diˈlibrət]
[54] [diˈlibəreit(id)]

22. The girl students live in a *separate*[55] part of the college, which is *separated*[56] from the main building by a wall.

[55] [ˈseprət]
[56] [ˈsepəreit(id)]

23. The doctor *advised*[57] him not to smoke too much, but he did not follow the doctor's *advice*[58].

[57] [ədˈvaiz(d)]
[58] [ədˈvais]

24. He is always *devising*[59] ways and means of getting money. Up to now his *devices*[60] have been failures.

[59] [diˈvaiz(iŋ)]
[60] [diˈvais(iz)]

25. Are all shops *closed*[61] today? – They are *close*[62] friends.

[61] [kləuz(d)] [62] [kləus]

26. Please *excuse*[63] me. – That is no good *excuse*[64].

[63] [ikˈskjuːz] [64] [ikˈskjuːs]

27. These parts of the machine must be *greased*[65] twice a day. There is a tin of *grease*[66] on the shelf.

[65] [griːz(d), griːs(t)]
[66] [griːs]

28. Do they still *use*[67] such an old instrument? No, it has been out of *use*[68] for a long time.

[67] [juːz]
[68] [juːs]

29. The officer was found guilty of *abuse*[69] of authority. – He *abused*[70] the confidence we placed in him.

[69] [əˈbjuːs]
[70] [əˈbjuːz(d)]

42 C. Pronunciation of Selected Names

Read aloud (after you have read aloud the English words in § 42 of HOW TO AVOID MISTAKES).

Great Britain

1. *Plymouth*[1], *Bournemouth*[2], *Southampton*[3], *Portsmouth*[4] and *Folkstone*[5] are on the south coast of England.
[1]['pliməθ] [2]['bɔ:nməθ] [3][sauθ'æm(p)tən] [4]['pɔ'tsməθ] [5]['fəukstən]

2. The easiest way from Germany to England is to go by boat from Bremerhaven to *Harwich*[6].
[6]['hæridʒ]

3. *Windsor*[7] lies on the *Thames*[8].
[7]['winzə] [8][temz]

4. *Greenwich*[9] Time is the mean time for the meridian of *Greenwich*[9].
[9]['gri:nidʒ]

5. There are famous old cathedrals in *Durham*[10], *Lincoln*[11] and *Gloucester*[12]. The new cathedral of *Coventry*[13] is an outstanding example of modern architecture.
[10]['dʌrəm] [11]['liŋkən] [12]['glɔstə] [13]['kɔvəntri]

6. *Edinburgh*[14] is the capital and *Glasgow*[15] the largest city of Scotland.
[14]['edinb(ə)rə] [15]['glɑ:sgəu]

7. The *Derby*[16] is the most famous English horserace; it takes place at Epsom on the first Wednesday in June.
[16]['dɑ:bi]

8. Oxford and *Cambridge*[17] are the two oldest English universities.
[17]['keimbridʒ]

9. *Warwick*[18] is a historic town in the West Midlands with several old buildings e.g. the two town gates, Lord *Leycester*'s[19] Hospital and above all *Warwick*[18] Castle.
[18]['wɔrik] [19]['lestə]

10. *Worcester*[20] sauce was first made at *Worcester*[20]. – *Cheshire*[21] cheese is a kind of cheese originally made in *Cheshire*[21].
[20]['wustə] [21]['tʃeʃə]

11. There was a young lady of *Gloucester*[22],
  Whose friends quite thought they had lost her,
    When her handbag they spied
    Coming back from a ride
  On the horns of a bull that had tossed her.
[22]['glɔstə]

12. An impertinent fellow of *Leicester*[23]
  Met a lady, and thus he addreicester:
    'Let my arms be a neicest
    Where your head, love, may reicest.'
  So she ran to his breicest, where he preicester.
[23]['lestə]

U.S.A.

13. *Connecticut*[1] and *Massachusetts*[2] are New England States; *Arkansas*[3] and *Tennessee*[4] are in the South, *Illinois*[5], *Michigan*[6] and *Missouri*[7] in the Middle West.
[1][kə'netikət] [2][ˌmæsə'tʃu:sits] [3]['ɑ:kənsɔ:] [4][ˌtenə'si:] [5][ˌilə'nɔi] [6]['miʃigən] [7][mi'zuəri]

14. *Chicago*[8] is one of the largest cities of the United States.
[8][ʃi'kɑ:gəu]

15. The *Gettysburg*[9] Address is the famous speech of Abraham *Lincoln*[10] delivered in Nov. 1863. It contains the phrase 'government of the people, by the people, for the people.'
[9]['getizbə:g] [10]['liŋkən]

16. The *Niagara*[11] Falls are over 150 ft. high.
[11][nai'ægərə]

17. *Harvard*[12] University is the oldest institution of higher learning in the United States; it was founded in 1636.
[12]['hɑ:vəd]

Germany

18. The Olympic Games of 1972 took place in *Munich*, the capital of *Bavaria*[2].	[1]['mjuːnik] [2][bə'vɛəriə]
19. George I was the first king of the House of *Hanover*[3].	[3]['hænəuvə]
20. The *Danube*[4] is one of the longest rivers of Europe[5].	[4]['dænjuːb] [5]['juərəp]
21. The *Moselle*[6] flows into the *Rhine*[7] at Coblenz[8].	[6][məu'zel] [7][rain]
22. *Cologne*[9] is one of the oldest German cities.	[8]['kəublents] [9][kə'ləun]

Europe

23. *Athens*[1] is the capital of *Greece*[2], *Brussels*[3] of *Belgium*[4], *Copenhagen*[5] of Denmark, *Prague*[6] of Czechoslovakia[7], *Rome*[8] of Italy, *Vienna*[9] of Austria[10], Dublin of *Eire*[11].	[1]['æθinz] [2][griːs] [3]['brʌslz] [4]['beldʒəm] [5][kəupn'heig(ə)n] [6][prɑːg] [7]['tʃekəu-slə'vækiə] [8][rəum] [9][vi'ənə] [10]['ɔstriə, *Am.* 'ɔː ~] [11]['ɛərə]
24. *Malta*[12] and *Cyprus*[13] are islands in the *Mediterranean*[14].	[12]['mɔːltə] [13]['saiprəs] [14][ˌmeditə'reiniən]
25. *Venice*[15], *Florence*[16] and *Naples*[17] are famous Italian cities.	[15]['venis] [16]['flɔrəns] [17]['neiplz]
26. *Geneva*[18] was the seat of the League[19] of Nations.	[18][dʒi'niːvə] [19][liːg]
27. *Gibraltar*[20] has been a British possession since 1904.	[20][dʒi'brɔːltə]
28. By hovercraft[21] you can cross the Channel from *Calais*[22] to Ramsgate in 40 minutes.	[21]['hɔvəkrɑːft] [22]['kælei]

Other Continents

29. The *Ganges*[1] flows from the *Himalaya*[2] to the Bay of Bengal[3]. *Calcutta*[4] is a large city in the *Ganges*[1] Delta.	[1]['gændʒiːz] [2][ˌhimə'leiə] [3][beŋ'gɔːl] [4][kæl'kʌtə]
30. It will be very difficult to find an agreement between *Israel*[5] and *Egypt*[6].	[5]['izrei(ə)l] [6]['iːdʒipt]
31. The Soviet[7] Union *(Russia*[8]*)*, China, *Japan*[8], India, *Pakistan*[10], Sri Lanka[11] *(Ceylon*[12]*)*, Iran *(Persia*[13]*)*, Turkey, Indonesia and the *Philippines*[14] are the largest countries of *Asia*[15].	[7]['səuviət] [8]['rʌʃə] [9][dʒə'pæn] [10][ˌpɑːki'stɑːn] [11][ˌsri'læŋkə] [12][si'lɔn] [13]['pəːʃə, *Am.* ʒ] [14]['filipiːnz] [15]['eiʃə, *Am.* 'eiʒə]
32. Delhi [16] is the capital of India; *Peking*[17] is the capital of China.	[16]['deli] [17]['piːkiŋ]

Christian and Other Names

33. Christian names: (male) *Adam*[1], *Albert*[2], *Andrew*[3], *Anthony*[4], *Archibald*[5], *Graham*[6], *Matthew*[7], *Michael*[8], *Philip*[9], *Sean*[10]*;* (female) *Agatha*[11], *Alice*[12], *Eve*[13], *Jean*[14], *Joan*[15].	[1]['ædəm] [2]['ælbət] [3]['ændruː] [4]['æntəni] [5]['ɑːtʃibəld] [6]['greiəm] [7]['mæθjuː] [8]['maikl] [9]['filip] [10][ʃɔːn] [11]['ægəθə] [12]['ælis] [13][iːv] [14][dʒiːn] [15][dʒəun]
34. Surnames: *Douglas*[16], *Guinness*[17], *Wallace*[18].	[16]['dʌgləs] [17]['ginis] [18]['wɔlis]
35. *Berkeley*[19] is a surname. The city of *Berkeley*[20] on San Francisco Bay, the location of the University of California, was named after the Irish philosopher George *Berkeley*[19] (1685–1753).	[19]['bɑːkli] [20]['bəːkli]
36. *St Augustine*[21] (first archbishop of Canterbury, led the mission to England from Rome).	[21][ɔː'gʌstin]

37. Anne *Boleyn*[22] (second wife of Henry VIII)	[22][ˈbulin]
38. *Canute*[23] (Danish king of England, 1016–1035)	[23][kəˈnjuːt]
39. *Geoffrey Chaucer*[24] (English poet, author of the 'Canterbury Tales', 1340–1400)	[24][ˈdʒefri ˈtʃɔːsə]
40. Robinson *Crusoe*[25] (hero of a novel by Daniel Defoe, 1719)	[25][ˈkruːsəu]
41. Sir John *Falstaff*[26] (person in Shakespeare's 'Henry IV' and 'The Merry Wives of Windsor[27]')	[26][ˈfɔːlstɑːf] [27][ˈwinzə]
42. *Gulliver's*[28] Travels (novel by Jonathan[29] Swift, 1726)	[28][ˈgʌlivə] [29][ˈdʒɔnəθən]
43. *Guy Fawkes*[30] (one of the conspirators against James I, Guy Fawkes's Day: 5th Nov.)	[30][ˈgai ˈfɔːks]
44. Sherlock *Holmes*[31] (private detective, hero of a number of detective stories by Conan Doyle)	[31][ˈʃəːlɔk ˈhəumz]
45. *Abraham Lincoln*[32] (American President, 1809–1865)	[32][ˈliŋkən]
46. William Somerset *Maugham*[33] (English dramatist and novelist, 1874–1965)	[33][mɔːm]
47. James *Monroe*[34] (American president, 1758–1831, 'Monroe Doctrine')	[34][mənˈrəu]
48. Sir Walter *Raleigh*[35] (Engl. courtier, soldier, colonizer, 1552–1618)	[35][ˈrɔːli, ˈræli]
49. *Ulysses*[36] (legendary king of Ithaca[37])	[36][juːˈlisiːz] [37][ˈiθəkə]

II. SPELLING

A. Difficult Words

1. Frequently Confused Words

43

Which is correct? Put in the missing letters and write the whole words on a worksheet.

a) a *or* **e**?

1. The mayor __ccepted all the offers, __xcept the last. 2. He eats and drinks to __xcess. – The only __ccess to the castle was over a drawbridge. 3. There was a s__cret door in the wall. – Cows are s__cred in India. 4. He made every __ffort to earn more money, but in spite of that he cannot __fford a holiday this summer. 5. My uncle's house is bigger th__n my father's. – Let's eat and th__n go for a walk. 6. We wish you a m__rry Christmas. – They will m__rry at Easter. 7. These measures will __ffect trade and commerce, they will have an __ffect on the whole economic situation. We hope that they will __ffect a complete change.

b) ea *or* **ee**?

1. The tree does not b__r fruit any longer. – Which do you prefer, b__r or wine? – There are four brown b__rs in the zoo. 2. Do you like your tea sw__t? – The smith wiped the sw__t from his dirty forehead. 3. The gr__t man was gr__ted with applause. 4. At the end of his sp__ch he began to sp__k about the future of British industry. 5. D__ds are better than words. – His father was d__d. 6. P__rs are members of the House of Lords. – Apples and p__rs are cheap this year.

c) e *or* **not**?

1. Please put the letter into the envelop__. 2. Do you like champagn__? 3. The tree has not born__ fruit for years. 4. He held his breath__ in excitement. 5. Let's go for a bath__ in the river. 6. Britain helped her former colonies in the develop__ment of their industry. 7. The old soldier had taken part in several campaign__s in different parts of the empire. 8. The visitors came in their national costum__s. 9. What is the h__ight of the television tower in London? 10. Mother must prepar__ the meal now. 11. It is the custom__ in England to queue up at the bus stop. 12. You are qui__t__ right. – Keep qui__t__. 13. The policeman s__ized the thief by the collar. 14. In the Statut__ of Westminister the equality of status of the Dominions was recognized by Britain.

d) e *or* **. .**?

1. The city counc__l followed the couns__l of the mayor. 2. The d__ceased left a wife and four children; he died of an incurable d__sease. 3. We shan't pr__ceed in this work. 4. An officer of the guard pr__ceded the queen.

e) oa, oo, ou, au *or* **. .**?

1. In the c__rse of the inquiries the police found out the real c__se of his hatred. 2. The ship sailed along the c__st. 3. Don't l__se that money. – Shall we l__se the dog? 4. John is a good g__lkeeper. – The thief was sent to g__l for three years. 5. There were gr__ps of people standing around. – Tr__ps of soldiers marched through the village. 6. The fog was as thick as pea s__p. – A bar of s__p. 7. That remark r__sed his anger, and he r__sed his hand as if to strike her.

f) shirt *or* **skirt,** *etc.?*

1. Which is more expensive, a woman's s__irt or a man's s__irt? 2. *(Kanal)* The English C________l joins the Atlantic and the North Sea, the Panama C________l the Atlantic and the Pacific. 3. The ma__or of the town, several government offic____s, a ma__or and some other offic____s of the Guards took part in the banquet. 4. A man who betr____s his country is a tr____tor. Tr____son is a capital offence. 5. That senten__e does not make any sen__e. – He had a wonderful time at his father's expen__e. 6. At l____st he made up his mind to buy the boat; it will cost him at l___st £ 60 to have it rep____red.

g) Just for Fun

Young sailor: "On my last voyage I saw waves forty feet h____gh."
Old sailor: "I was at sea for fifty years and never saw them that h____ght."
Young sailor: "Well, all is h____gher than it used to be. Look at the price for whisky for instance."

44,45 **2. Words with Special Consonants**

Which is correct? Put in the missing letters and write the whole words on a worksheet.

a) One or two consonants?

1. **c** su__ess, a__use, ne__essary, o__asion, a__ustom, o__ur, a__ount, a__ompany
2. **d** a__ress, sha__ow, wi__ow, go__ess
3. **l** para__e__, mode__, ga__ery, a__one, rebe__, interva__, coo__y, ga__op, rea__y
4. **m** acco__odate, co__ittee, gra__ophone, telegra__, progra__e, i__ediate, i__igrate, pro__ise, i__ense
5. **n** ca__on, e__emy, priso__er, a__ounce, a__oy
6. **p** co__y, a__artment, a__ly, o__onent, wea__on, o__ortunity, a__ology, a__roach, disa__oint, o__ress
7. **r** ca__eer, he__ing, su__ound, occu__ence, bu__ial, e__ect, fu__ier, to emba__ass, inte__est, a__ive
8. **s** gla__, po__e__ion, di__appear, a__ent, bu__es, aggre__ion, di__olve, sci__ors, witne__, poi__on, to a__a__inate, nece__ary
9. **t** to a__ach, to a__ract, commi__ee, pla__form, bu__ler, a__itude, viole__

46 **b) Special consonants**

Translate the words in brackets into English and write them on a worksheet.

1. Last *(Herbst)* my *(Neffe)* made a *(Reise)* from a small *(Hafen)* in India *(geradewegs)* into the *(Dschungel)*. 2. Are you *(sicher)* that *(Whisky)* is made from *(Weizen)?* 3. *(Reim)* and *(Rhythmus)* alone do not make a poem. 4. The *(Gespenst)* hid in an old suit of *(Rüstung)* beside the *(Säule)* and *(pfiff)* when the baron came into the hall. 5. In spite of his *(schlau)* arguments the accused could not convince the *(Richter)*; so he was *(verurteilt)* to three years' hard labour. 6. While the *(feierliche Hymne)* was being played, a *(hochmütig)* official *(Regierungsbeamter)* *(flüsterte)* to his neighbour. 7. Though the farmer used his *(Peitsche)* and the horses pulled with all their *(Kraft)*, they were unable to get the heavy waggon up the steep road to the *(Brücke)*.

c) s *or* **c**? 47

1. Macbeth was much more affected by the witches' prophe__ies than Banquo, to whom they had prophe__ied that his children should be kings. 2. If you take your father's advi__e and practi__e two hours a day, you will soon be able to play the sonata. 3. We advi__e you never to leave your driving licen__e in the car. 4. The engineer devi__ed an excellent plan, but he was unable to put it into practi__e.

d) v *or* **f**? 48

1. The woman was relie__ed to hear that her son had arrived sa__e and sound. 2. It is my belie__ that such a li__ely young lady will be able to earn her li__elihood as an actress. 3. Three people were buried ali__e by an avalanche; two others could be sa__ed. 4. "Li__e in London," a li__e broadcast on Radio One. 5. The police inspector got a bullet-proo__ jacket, but it pro__ed to be useless. 6. If you have sa__ed a lot of money, it is sa__est in the sa__e of a bank. 7. My uncle li__es a quiet li__e in the country. 8. Please belie__e me that he is innocent. There isn't any proo__ that he was in the bank that evening. 9. We must send relie__ to the refugees.

e) Mistakes? 46–49

Which of the three words is spelt incorrectly?

1. whether, straight, strenght
2. charakter, victuals, object
3. judge, brigde, shepherd
4. goverment, harvest, to damn
5. proof, safety, reproduktion
6. belief, to prophecy, ghost

3. Words with Special Vowels

Which is correct? Put in the missing letters and write the whole words on a worksheet.

a) Special vowels 50

1. **a** *or* **e**? mess__nger, pass__ge, marm__lade, sep__rate, cl__rk, assist__nt, comp__rative, sal__ry, p__rfume

2. **e, é, ee** *or* **nothing**? pig__on, apart__ment, caf__, employ__, ni__ce, serg__ant, ther__for__, compart__ment, committ__, fianc__, to issu__, good-by__, volunt__r, madam__, pr__cis, volum__, wher__ever, automobil__, magazin__, queu__, medicin__

3. **i** *or* **y**? tax__, st__le, l__eutenant, b__c__cle, m__ster__, cho__r

4. **a** *or* **o**? am__ng, t__bacco, c__coa

5. *What is missing?* to ende__vour, brill__ant, parl__ament, rece__pt, d__uble, bisc__it, sub__rb, ball__n, ju__ce, e__rnest, lett__ce

b) One *or* **two vowels**? 51

1. The pron__nciation was not correct; please, rep__t the word. 2. Can you expl__n this surprising excl__mation to us? You owe us an expl__nation. 3. Do you know how to pron__nce the words 'maint__nance' and 'sust__nance'? 4. The end of rep__ration payments was procl__med. 5. My shoes need rep__ring. 6. Constant rep__tition is necessary if you want to be successful.

52 **c) ei** *or* **ie**?

1. The policeman s__zed the th__f by the collar. 2. My n__ce shr__ked when she perc__ved the spider on the c__ling. 3. Many soldiers were sent to the rel__f of the bes__ged town. 4. When the oldest ch__f of the negroes had promised to make peace and the warriors had given their approval by banging their spears upon their sh__lds, the white men had ach__ved a bloodless victory. 5. You are dec__ving yourself if you bel__ve such a foolish thing.

4. Verbs and Numbers

Translate the words in brackets into English and write them on a worksheet.

53 **a) Verbs**

1. He l__ *(legte)* the book on the table. – The book always *(lag)* on the table. 2. She had *(gelegen)* in the grass for hours. She had l__ *(gelegt)* the book beside her. 3. Mr Lee *(vermietete)* the house to us. We *(bezahlen)* £ 45 a month. 4. Children who had *(gespielt)* near the house were *(gerissen)* out of the arms of their mothers by the cruel soldiers. 5. She *(setzte sich)* up in bed and *(hielt)* her breath when she *(hörte)* that something had *(gefallen)* off the table. She *(fühlte)* her heart beating. When the key *(fiel)* on the floor, she *(floh)* out of the room. 6. We *(flogen)* from Calais to Dover; together with us our car was *(geflogen)* across the Channel. 7. The boy *(setzte sich)* down at the table and *(wählte)* the biggest apple.

54 **b) Numbers**

Write in words: 440, 814, 515, 954, 418.
John was the (9.) out of (12). The (12.) and last was George.

5. Frequently Confused Prefixes and Suffixes

Which is correct? Put in the missing letters and write the whole words on a worksheet.

56 **a) Prefixes**

1. **e** *or* **i**? to d__vide, to d__cline, to d__crease, to d__gest, to d__fine, to d__cide, to d__vorce, to d__lay, to d__minish; to d__spair, to d__stroy, to d__scover, to d__sobey, to d__scribe, to d__stinguish, to d__spise

2. **c** *or* **not**? ex__ellent, ex__ample, ex__amination, ex__ess, ex__ept, to ex__ite, to ex__aggerate

3. **e** *or* **not**? befor__, to for__get, for__cast, for__head, for__ward, for__word, to for__give, ther__for__

4. **e** *or* **u**? to p__rsist, to p__rsue, to p__rchase, to p__rceive, to p__rform, p__rpose, p__rsuit, p__rsecution

57 **b) Suffixes: -able** *or* **-ible**?

1. invinc__ble, pay__ble, regrett__ble, not__ble, respons__ble, intellig__ble, reli__ble, inevit__ble, eat__ble, ed__ble, vis__ble, consider__ble

2. *Add* **-able** *or* **-ible** *to the following words, making any necessary changes in spelling:* favour, value, force, agree, comprehend, convert, desire, pity, access, suit, advise

c) Suffixes: -ance, -ant *or* **-ence, -ent**? 58

1. conveni_nt, appear_nce, acquaint_nce, viol_nt, signific_nt, magnific_nt, suffici_nt, disturb_nce, insol_nt, insur_nce, inherit_nce, evid_nce, griev_nce, urg_nt

2. *Add* **-ance** *or* **-ence** *to the following words, making any necessary changes in spelling:* attend, assist, depend, resemble, rely, accept, admit, insist, precede, occur, observe, resist

d) Suffixes: -ar, -er *or* **-or**? 59

1. bachel_r, labour_r, tail_r, trait_r, fri_r, wait_r, conduct_r, paint_r, spectat_r, emper_r, lawy_r, driv_r, ancest_r, doct_r

2. *Add* **-ar, -er** *or* **-or** *to the following words, making any necessary changes in spelling:* examine, success, conquer, beg, employ, govern, lie *(lügen)*, war, create, school, orate, sail, translate, visit, murder, interpret, explore, elevate, administrate

e) Suffixes: -ize *or* **-ise**? 60

1. to bapti_e, to organi_e, to adverti_e, to exerci_e, to reali_e, to coloni_e, to surpri_e, to critici_e, to improvi_e, enterpri_e, to symboli_e, to recogni_e, to summari_e

2. *Add* **-ize** (*or* **-ise**?) *to the following words, making any necessary changes in spelling:* general, actual, legal, drama, apology, equal, subsidy, economy, terror, sympathy

B. Spelling of Inflected and Derived Forms

1. Final Silent -e 61

e *or* **not**? *Add the endings to the following words:* rescu–ing, nine–th, nine–ty, canoe–ing, please–ant, peace–ful, awe–some, awe–ful, move–able, move–ment, service–able, argue–ment, refuse–al, noise–less, noise–y, agree–able, true–ly, behave–iour, grace–ious, trace–ing, abridge–ment, replace–able, malice–ious, blue–ish, active–ity, sincere–ly, assure–ance, safe–ty, fortune–ate, grieve–ance, queue–ing, please–ure, manage–able, whole–ly, advertise–ment, miserable–ly, arrange–ment, notice–ing, immune–ity, imagine–able, shape–less, shave–ing, whole–some

2. Final -y 62

a) y *or* **i**? *Add the endings to the following words:* history–cal, joy–ous, easy–est, lonely–ness, pretty–ly, pay–ment, marry–age, die–ing, day–ly, sly–ness, lady–like, bury–al, glory–ous, penny–less, try–al, accompany–ment, mercy–ful, rely–able, annoy–ance

b) *Write the present and past participles of the following verbs:* to try, to tie, to annoy, to hurry, to die, to dry, to play, to pay, to lie, to lay, to bury, to employ, to say, to buy, to qualify, to obey, to worry, to fry

c) *Give the plural or the third person singular of the simple present tense:* chimney, fly, lady, day, reply, valley, story, alley, monkey, enemy, city; to try, to betray, to deny, to pray, to bury, to annoy

63,64

3. Final -o + s and -f + s

a) *Put the following words into the plural:* hero, photo, potato, cargo, piano, negro, dynamo, tomato, veto, credo, radio, torpedo, echo

b) *Put the following words into the plural:* roof, calf, shelf, life, half, loaf, safe, knife, wolf, dwarf, wife, proof, cliff, thief, chief

c) *Put the words in brackets into the plural.*
1. The *(chief)* of the *(negro)* had several *(wife)*. 2. The *(roof)* of quite a number of houses were destroyed, and several people lost their *(life)*. 3. The *(thief)* even searched the books on the *(shelf)*. 4. In England people are allowed to cut *(potato)* with *(knife)*. 5. Two ships with valuable *(cargo)* got lost on the *(cliff)*. 6. Are these *(handkerchief)* or *(scarf)*? 7. The soldiers regarded *(himself)* as *(hero)*. 8. Some *(calf)* were torn by *(wolf)*. 9. He took some *(photo)* of the *(buffalo)*. 10. Please cut the *(tomato)* in *(half)*.

65

4. Doubling of Final Consonants

Double consonants or not? Write the correct words on a worksheet.

1. equip–ed, benefit–ing, hum–ing, admit–ance, wood–en, wet–est, sin–er, happen–ing, worship–er, visit–or, sweat–er, develop–ed, bus–es, drug–ist, thin–est, profit–able, gosip–ing, slip–ery, omit–ed, becom–ing, drop–ing, begin–er, flood–ed, swim–ing, hug–ing, brood–ing, plan–ed, commit–ed, ship–ing, profit–ing, hop–ing (2: to hope, to hop)

2. stir–ed, colour–ing, (to bar) bar–ed, roar–ing, confer–ence, confer–ing, refer–ence, fur–ier, cur–ed, prefer–ed, prepar–ed, confer–able, occur–ence, differ–ing, refer–ed, consider–ed, blur–ed, bor–ing, concur–ed, mar–ed, despair–ed, defer–ed, clear–ance, char–ed, cheer–ed, deter–ent, abhor–ence, declar–ed

3. shovel–ing, cruel–est, wool–en, sail–ed, cancel–ed, jewel–er, loyal–ist, patrol–ed, equal–ize, equal–ing, impel–ed, cool–ing, tunnel–ed, avail–able, rebel–ious, control–able, boil–ed, conceal–ed, compel–ed

66

5. Compound Words with -l

l *or* **ll**? farewe__, fu__, a__ways, a__ right, to fu__fi, unti__, we__come, wonderfu__, ski__, a__most, a__ together, ti__, ski__fu__, sma__ness, a__ready, a__together

*

What's the difference between a *jeweller* and a *jailer?* – One sells watches and the other watches cells.

C. Special Problems of Orthography

67

1. Capital Letters

Put capital letters in the correct places in the following sentences:

a) on july 1st, 1969, prince charles was invested as prince of wales at caernarvon castle. to the singing of 'god bless the prince of wales', the prince was conducted to the chamberlain tower, where he awaited the arrival of the queen and the duke of edinburgh. after they had taken seats on their thrones, documents creating him prince of wales were read in english and welsh, and during the welsh reading the queen invested her son with the insignia of his title.

b) once there was a great and powerful king, who had seven children, six sons and a beautiful daughter. one day, when the princess was alone in the park of the royal palace, she was abducted by the king of a neighbouring country. the six princes at once followed their sister, slew the abductor and brought her back to her father's palace.

c) queen elizabeth II is a descendant of the saxon king, egbert, who united all england in the year 829. according to the royal titles act of 1953, the royal title in the united kingdom is: elizabeth the second, by the grace of god of the united kingdom of great britain and northern ireland and of her other realms and territories queen, head of the commonwealth, defender of the faith.

d) the house of lords consists of the lords temporal and the lords spiritual. the lords spiritual are the archbishops of canterbury and york, the bishops of london, durham and winchester, and 21 other bishops of the church of england.

e) her majesty's government is the body of ministers charged for the time being with the administration of national affairs. the prime minister is appointed by the crown, and all other ministers are appointed by the crown on the recommendation of the prime minister. *(Britain, An Official Handbook, 1967)*

f) about thirty people were present at my grandfather's birthday party; among them, of course, father and mother, uncle george, aunt edith, several cousins of mine and also some of grandfather's friends: professor lee, sir bryan and lady garratt, colonel snell.

g) in a democratic country the government cannot have an arrested person held without bringing him before a magistrate with the least possible delay. – her majesty's government – st paul's cathedral – there are a lot of big cathedrals in england. – several new universities were built after the war, among them the university of sussex. – "storm in channel, continent isolated" – australia is the smallest continent. – new year's day is the first day of the year. – the northern part of manhattan with central park is laid out like a checkerboard. the streets run east and west, twenty to a mile, the avenues north and south, seven to a mile. – rockefeller center stretches for three blocks from 48th to 51st street, west of fifth avenue.

h) the sun rises in the east and sets in the west. – he spent some years in the east. – after long discussions we decided to travel west. – they moved from east anglia to south kensington. – he prefers scotch whisky to french brandy. – he started to learn german in may last year. – a french window serves as a window as well as a door. – to show one's feelings is un-english.

i) *(Headings and title of books, etc.)* this morning, this evening, so soon *(Baldwin)* – death the proud brother *(Wolfe)* – look back in anger *(Osborne)* – the old man and the sea *(Hemingway)* – a tale of two cities *(Dickens)* – the way of all flesh *(Butler)* – mourning becomes electra *(O'Neill)* – the skin of our teeth *(Wilder)* – who's afraid of virginia woolf *(Albee)* – to others than you *(Dylan Thomas)* – the lover tells of the rose in his heart *(W. B. Yeats)*

69

2. Hyphen

a) *Hyphen or one word without hyphen?*

to cross examine
post Shakespearian
co worker
extra ordinary
by plot
non sense
anti Christian
non violent
re appear
self explanatory
vice chairman
self evident

b) *Fill in the missing hyphens.*

a drive in restaurant
a face to face interview
a Secretary of State
my son in law
a second hand car
the washing up
catch as catch can
well to do people
blood red hands
an out of door exercise
a matter of fact
thirty one thirty thirds
my grown up daughter
a merry go round

c) *Change the phrases in italics into compound adjectives.*

Note: a girl *with fair hair* = a *fair-haired* girl
a dress *that fits well* = a *well-fitting* dress
a journey *of two hundred miles* = a *two-hundred-mile* journey
equipment *that is out of date* = *out-of-date* equipment

a man *with a long nose*
a boy *who is twelve years old*
a ticket *for the second class*
a river *that runs slow*
shoes *with high heels*
a play *that was well acted*
a vehicle *that moves fast*
ground *covered with snow*
an interval *of fifteen minutes*
a path *lined with trees*
a shark *that eats men*
a visit *that is worth while*
a person *of narrow mind*
ideas *that are up to date*
a mountain *of nine thousand feet*

70

3. Division of Words

a) *Divide the following words according to the first two rules on p. 53 of* HOW TO AVOID MISTAKES.
(Note: ch, ph, sh, th, tch *are treated as single consonants.)*

leather, children, public, pleasure, nephew, sugar, cradle, cushion, money, sacred, promise, nothing, bishop, trifle, kitchen, melody, needle, bachelor, progress, cousin, weapon, gather, woman, profit, moral, method, bugle

b) *Divide the following words according to word formation.*

without, subway, governess, beautiful, active, splitting, coming, falling, reading, shopping, higher, wetter, national, assistant, unhappy, farmer, postage, profitable, exclaim, almost, dustbin, specialize, getting, obtain, teacher, outside

c) *Divide the following words according to pronunciation. (Remember:* ch, ph, sh, th, tch *are treated as single consonants, but not* st.)

water, elephant, jacket, victor, rather, poem, fasten, seldom, pardon, worry, basket, neither,